"Picture Poems"
Prent Jie Dig

New Poetry Concept, Poems Written From Pictures

(English & Afrikaans Poems Combined)

Dawid Brink

"PICTURE POEMS" PRENTJIE DIG

New Poetry Concept,
Poems Written from Pictures

WORKBOOK PRESS
RECOMMENDED
LITERARY BOOK COMPETITION 2024

DAWID BRINK

WORKBOOK PRESS LLC
187 E Warm Springs Rd
Suite B285 Las Vegas NV 89119 USA

Website: https://workbookpress.com/
Hotline: 1-888-818-4856
Email: admin@workbookpress.com

Ordering Information:
Quantity sales. Special discounts are available on quantity purchases by corporations, associations, and others. For details, contact the publisher at the address above.

ISBN-13: 978-1-963718-21-8 (Paperback Version)
         978-1-963718-23-2 (Digital Version)

PUB. DATE: 11/24/2024

ACKNOWLEDGEMENT

My deepest appreciation to….

All those who encouraged me and helped me in prayer, project, and financial support to brink this book to completion.

I want to thank also my siblings; this book would not be complete without you.

Most importantly, my gratitude to the Lord and Savior Jesus for His grace and companionship during this project and the Holy Spirit's faithful guidance through this assignment.

INTRODUCTION

I was introduced to Facebook in 2010 and later on, started writing poems about pictures of friends and our interaction, also addressing battering and rape of women and children. I call these PICTURE POEMS starting a new poetry concept. Not writing a poem and search for a picture to fit the poem, but rather writing the poem from a picture. I hope you will all enjoy my book which has English and Afrikaans poems and dedicated pictures.

DISCLAIMER: All the pictures used inside the book were all granted permission by owners.

PART I: ENGLISH POEMS WITH UNIQUE PICTURES

DID WE GO WRONG..

O! Glorious God where did we go wrong... our song...
To Thee, Thee only did, did we truly long...
Our hearts mould in one, bold and strong...
Seeds of worldly cares...rattled our throng...

By and by did we loose our focus...
Satan's traps, stolen till all is hoaxes...
Jesus said truly, years eaten by locust...
To you...surely restored...in Kingdom focus!

Clutching desperate each other's throat...
Satan's joy...you...demon toy and evil gloat...
Abandoned lay Jesus' righteous coat...

Deep sighing, strong with tears in prayer so rare...
It's your loving spouse...she's, he's... the louse!

Demons ruling your houses, tiptoe silent as a mouse...
FAMILIES BRITTLE...STOP A LITTLE… LISTEN… BE AWARE!!!

God our Father's Throne Room's open wide...
Holy Spirit let Him rule you deep, deep ... INSIDE...

by Dawid Brink © pic Jorandey

GRACE A SWAN

Despair...like darkness deeper, deeper she grows...
Growling, fierce deep...deep down lows..
Grace-like swan...yet, yet steady she flows...
In life storms your glittery white a glows...
Don't you knows power-wave...you it throws...
Murky deep...deep so strong your foes...

Maul....Maul down, down, down indeed she goes...
Grass entangled, grips of fear, fear down belows...
Swallow you, you swallows Foes, hand feet and toes...

GRACE...IN STORM MY HEART BEATS...SLOWS...
He Glory King...even me...a Swan...HIM WE KNOWS...

by Dawid Brink ©

STORMER

Stormer...off! Chilly night on
thunderin hoof you'd go
Breathin fire-smoke, very fast not pacin slow...
Moon on beams dimmery down you glow...
Ice and cold to where foggy rivers flow...
My love, love do you really, really know??

That hazy misty blur your hasty...way?
Darkest night! O! Love won't you stay...
Songs...words of soothin love...if you may...
Sure darkness...if you may...danger games you play...

Thunderin hoof splits the dreary saddest night...
O! O! Stay...this disastrous flight!
O! O! OOO...May ! ...you know...you is...right!
Darkest...O !..night! Will you win this fight...
You !...O! Love...return your flight...to LIGHT?

by Dawid Brink © pic Heintj

THE SPIRIT, BRIDE and ME
(the day is gone far, night..)

LORD NOW!! We answer Thy call...
By Thy O! Spirit Thy enemies O! Lord do fall...
Both now foul evil spirits ugly and tall...
Brace with Love, Power and Grace our only wall!

Bride...beautiful...His Bride now's no time to hide...
Strengthen You WILL O! STRONG SPIRIT...by my side.
Holiness, Goodness, Joy sublime...also mine...
Faithfulness...Power in the hour...also thine...

Wisdom-knowledge ...visions reveling my position
Clearing Thy way...for me Stay my Mission...
Healing...Miracles... drive demon infirmities away
Kingdom Victories..all in Thy Word to stay...

YaHuSHua Ha' MASHIACH's victory Throne...you His very own...
His enemies, underfoot...this ALL in HEAVEN and EARTH is
KNOWN!!!

by Dawid Brink ©

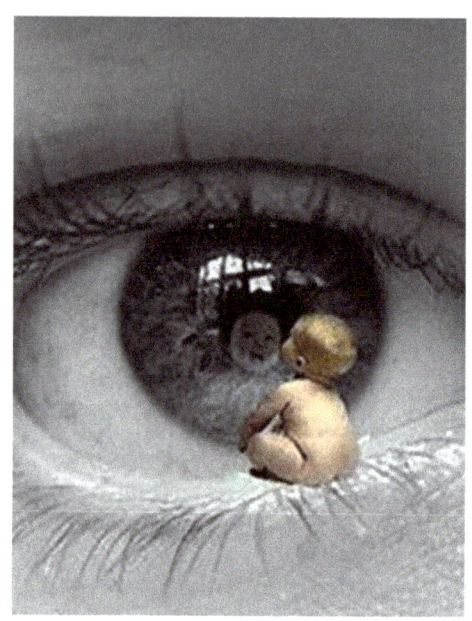

HIS EYE ON ME

Like babe's in vision His eye...
Safe from fears...safe we lie
A vision... open my spirit-heart...
All drear...death and darkness'll part!

HIS EYE...sees big and tall...
Yes! You!...even in the Mall.
Kings...Queens, beauties in a hall...
Witches driving...disobedient...king of Saul.

Yes! You!...Yes you the apple of His Eye..
Death.. O! Jesus...you still ask why?

To Kingly Palace...raised high from filt~sty..
Amazement, break silent...strongly shout...O! My!

HIS GLORY shown to me...His revelation will start...
Wide all open the eyes of my heart...
You'll still see the splinters..deep in...mine...
Maybe a stake...cross stuck...deeper in thine...??

by Dawid Brink ©

LOVE on a TREE

Chipmunks climbing a tree
Up and down, three by three..
Which one could be me?

Love miles and miles by the hour
To all the girls O! so fair...a flower..
With love Praises Thee we...shower!

He did, did He die on a tree
Shedding Precious Blood..He on me..
Openly...all world's could see

Could my hand...hand Him a...flower?
Souls, souls dreary shut tight in tower
Released from...demon-power??

Father with All Love, me He'd shower...
All His Son's petrels...night hour... A broken flower!!!

by Dawid Brink
© pic Jorandey

COLOR...KALEIDOSCOPE

*'Captured Inside a Phantasmagoria Kaleidoscope of
Engorged Glorious Colors..
.Star Streamed Refractive HMMMM...YummY!'...STAR*

*Brilliant...Gorgeous Kaleidoscope...colors mix...
Put your and my painted world in a fix...
Playing straight and skew our color...stix...*

*Red...Yellow...Black...White, Grey and Blue...
Paul...Peter...Maggie....Judas you and a girl named Sue?
Mine is Pink...Lilac...Yellows...Rosy...Which is you??*

*Untangled bound by Covenant Rainbow...Once?
God...you and me...Took firmly...their Stanz...*

by Dawid Brink © pic & quote Star

MAGGIE…a LOVELY BOOK to READ

(ALL mothers & wives) Happy Mothers Day

She…has a cover so exquisite
She…n glimpse so gorgeous!
Brown…Darker Brown…Blond…and…Red
Streaks of dazzling tints…
Green windows in kaleidoscope brilliance

Feeling size and shape in my hands…perfect…
From cover…to…cover…
More perfect…than…exquisite perfect…
From cover…to…cover…

Bold, yet almost…fragile picture

Pasted on volumes and volumes of...
Intriguing...passionate revelations
To be paged one...by...one... by me?

Hair raizzzing stories...some...
Some Draw strong tears from my eyes

Tender taints of fluttering love.
Jump out at you, from this page...
Child chapters from early youth
Two handsome boy chapters...girl chapter
Words of pride and...grace...She...
Flutter from these pages

MOTHERHOOD CHAPTER......
Deep gratitude....love tender...chapters
Respect washed with grace
Descends...deep, deep and lay in a heart

Laughter builds bubbly....
To tingling contagious excitement!
From these pages...my love
Hundred years still to short
Revealing all those treasured depths...
OF THIS BOOK....MAGGIE....
I...I...Love to read!!

By: Dawid Brink 2002 © pic Star

MORNING DEW…in BLOOM

Fresshhh!...Fresh dewdrops on my velvet's open wide
Feed me! O! Feed my crimson tide...
Bugs and bees...spiders...Ha! My flower does hide...
Sweet nectar deep-sweetness inside...

Brightly my lilac colour display in softly rain...
Prague...the Fair...or....a grave in Spain..
Whichever way I stay...or...is lain
Intrigue king and pauper insane...

On Queens beauti, or...dirty castle wall...
Or...even foul buildings rising tall...
I'm sold at the mall..even...at every stall...
Young handsomest;s gift to lovely a girl...small...

My glorious fragrance graces king's hall...
Do you reek my friend, when ground and maul..??..

by Dawid Brink © pic Enrico

DANGER PATHS

Do...you...know!...the...heart's path..?
That makes you trickle and laugh...
Joy unspeakable and happy...Satiated hearts...

Squashed by careless feet in the dirt..
How awefull!...sore...the pain and hurt..
SQUASHED RAW...now will you be the third?
Fluttering...wounded like a bird...

How...dooo...you sleep cozy at night?
From where you plan and launch your fight...
You said you wouldn't leave...
STILL!...STILL!!...WAS I SO, SO UTTERLY DECEIVE..?

Out of the cold, cold snowy heart...
YES! YES!! Out I go...THAT's a START!!!
Soaring high and strong...the...eagle fly..
Searching...true love that never die!!!

Somewhere out there...there…is… a heart...
That will never trample...trample...me apart?
Back over the moon we shall fly!
Stronger...Wiser...You...and...I..

by Dawid Brink © pic by Zetti

THE 'GOOD' FIGHT of FAITH
(1 Tim 6:12; Phil 3:7~14)

Soldiers so strong and fair...
TAKE THEM, STURDY ON!!!...in pair...
Finally men...of old...Fought strong and bold!
There...lay God's Champ in the ring...
Bruise...scared to death he'd bring...
Marks of JESUS his body sing...
Angels Praises!!! Where is the sting??
Third heaven he there saw...
Things to glorious...stand he in AWE!!!
Yet to life restore, to battle once more!!
Heaven's choir... PRAISE TO HIM!! they ROAR!!!
Nero cruelly snuffed out his righteous given life...
Couldn't end God's Champs soul's strife...
He fought the 'GOOD FIGHT' of faith...
AT LAST IN FATHER's ARMS...Paul is SAFE....

by Dawid Brink © pic Yann

NIGHT CAME

Multitudes!!..Multitudes in the valley of decision??
Million die! Millions DIE!! No Kingdom vision!!!
Who will go! WHO WILL GO WITH THE MISSION???

Light...in...you...could be utterly darkness... growing?
Reap! REAP!! Soul...what you're really sowing..
Life line to you we throw...just, just bend alowing?

Night! ... O! Night couldn't you stay???
King our Groom...Jesus...well on the way!!!
Glorious Bride...WAKE-UP and PRAY!!!
KEEP FOUL, EVIL SPIRITS AT BAY!

If when we no longer could work the day...
THEN NIGHT RUSHES IN...OUT COMES EVIL to PLAY...

by Dawid Brink © pic Rhonda

KIMBERYAH's VICTORY

KimberYAH's...Fierce battle cry..
'IN JESUS NAME you'll DIE !!!
Deepest hell, back demon fly !!!
JESUS BLOOD...WORD and SWORD...said I !!!

Few soldiers with courage left in this fight.
Yielding shield and sword with might...
Battle on though the night to early light...
Jesus's mighty army clear in sight!

Battle on sweet Lady fair...
Use sword and shield will protect to tear
Salvation's helm keep safe thy hair...
Kingdoms armor is strong to wear!!!

Deep prayer...sweat...her eye does close...
With strength to Thee her song arose...
10,000 glorious mighty blows...
Brings her!! .. New demon rows!!!

by Dawid Brink © pic by Yann

LIFE SILOUETTE's

Figures caught in crimson-blue sun...
Silhouette's with faces...nun
Each frozen...eternal pose...
Warm colors...blue and rose...

Which one's yours in time?
Make thy life truly rhyme...
My sunset...my dawn...my life?
Through depth's...hell, joy...strife

First stanza, living laughter fun...
Then! ...aching pain, want to run
a STOP! Lost in time is fine
But Who chooses silhouetted line?

Time, pure, deep reflection's dance...
Life deepest end...my true's t stance...

by Dawid Brink © pic by Star

MICHAEL

Michael, Arc Angel big, tall and SO strong!!
'Where'?... Where were you so long?
Daniel confessing sins of them all...
Echos of great passion...down God's big Hall!

Since the cruel cross, Jesus reign!
Yes! Yes!! I'll make it plain!
Satan's dirty dragon hoard.
Their 'skin & scalp' Jesus scored!!!

His Angel-force...yes...and I
Strong the Mighty, they fly...
War in heaven did he make,
All Jesus 'scalps' he'd take!!

No more accuser there!!!
Only Father, Son and Spirit fair...
HALLELUJAH!!! HIS PRAISES RING!!!

ALL OUR VOICES JOIN...HEAVEN CHOIR SING!!!

HALLELUJAH! HALLELUJAH!!
HALLELUJAH!!! RING!!!!!!!!

THE BLOOD SHALL PREVAIL!

by Dawid Brink © pic Star~lite

WE SPOKE...THY LIGHT?

My Child, Lovely you are! Winner by far!
Father, My...patience fell...
Heart weighed, O in hell...

My Child, All! All!! IS paid!
In Jesus, You...on cross it was laid!!
Father, my world know it well
Sin I even will, all will tell...

My Child, find you in my Son
Death, sin...hell, He'd won!!
Father, I believe Thy sturdy word!
2,000 years, echos I have heard..

My Child, your Holy Righteousness, My only Son!
Father, Three in One!!
Praise God the old man IS FINALLY WON!!!

by Dawid Brink © pic by Paris

SHALL we DANCE?

To you my Love, I bow…
Take my hand and now...
Glide on stary sky...
Over glittery moon thy lye

Float...Butterfly, Butterfly...Float
Hear their ch-eerie laughter...and do gloat...
Come with me, sail away my boat!
On live seas...away, away we float...

Your Royal beauty and favoured grace...
Keep my toe and foe in place
Come away my Love to lovelier place?
So I could complete my race!

This circle may it never end...
Your heart NeverNeverLand to send!!!

by Dawid Brink © pic Lizette

THE ROCK and WATER

Lord O! Lord!... pull my hand!
On you O! Solid Rock I stand...
Through cross and nailing hand...
I'll follow brief... brief and hollow...
My cross upside down we'll follow!!

Breach far and wide,.. Thy Crimson tide...
Let me bathe and hide...deep and wide...
O! Sea of Holy Blood a fore us go...
Bow to Him deep and low!

Calm the seas He can...
Broken dreams of every man!!!

by Dawid Brink ©

MAN IN THE SHOWER

(specially for broken shower.. Con)
Splash me! ...wash me! ...thy cooling breath...
Touch me all over! ...now in all power!!
Yes! Yes! Man from my shower!!

His open mouth water and glissning oil...out it throw...
Refresh.. .revitelise ...splashing blow...
Spray thick and slow- it flow...

My head, bod...face and... O!
Tell me refreshing head...GO!
MAN OOFFF MY SHOWER...SLOW!!!

I believe...really...really she should!
Hold me...like...she...should! Aaa!

by Dawid Brink © pic Connie Kapp

THREE CROSS and a LIGHT

Three crosses fade the misty sky...
Simon Peter! Simon Peter! Did Jesus lie..?
Down..Death...in His tomb
His mother born Him out her womb!

Bitter her's and Mary, from Dala's tears they cry...
DEAD! DEAD!! ...they ask why?
In my arms on bosom, He'd lye..
SHAKE HIM! Shake hhimm... O! Why he'd die??
Yet! He arose...first light!
Three days, three nights...with might...
Broken prison walls...Death-Victor fight...
PRAISE!!! PRAISE!!! Man and host He made right?

IN HEAVEN...YET GLORIOUS LIGHT...
HE...WAS TAKEN...to HIS FATHER SIGHT!!!

by Dawid Brink © pic by Darre

INNER CORE

Deep...Deep Rise my Inner Core...
Him, Him I do only adore!!
He, He made through my heart's door...
Deep...Deep through my Inner Core!

Wicked this heart of mine!
Does and will really shine...
Washed in His Blood...
Cleanst soul-spirit' from dirty muud!

evil, evil deep was my inner core...
Satan's hoard, we friends...their inner store...
Till Jesus...I see on the cross He bore...
All my sin and inner gore!!

Radiance... face and core!!
Death to sin child within I roar!!!

He there reign as King, and He is proud...
Praise God and shout aloud!!!

Now Deep my Deep in-store...
He...only He, rule my INNER CORE!!!

by Dawid Brink
© pic by Ninna via Star

LIGHT CAME

In the early night's chill...so chill...
My heart sure it's very, very still....
Head and shoulder, why look down?
Is he, he still in town??

Alas!! The angry fight!
Will he leave at first light??
O! My heart it's lone...I know! Be strong!
How! A where did we wrong??

The chill in my bone, is it still?
Yet! For my part he will!
A light bright...stop the fight!
Love he me still? Yes! Yes!! Be sure He be might!!!

Assured, be matured...he will...
Cherish love and adore...me still...

In the chill of night, bright is the light...
Yes! Yes!! Be sure, sure he is right??

by Dawid Brink
© pic Ninna

KERNEELS

Snugglely...so to sleep, paw under a jaw...
a Mouse once no trice, its a froggg at pillows End?
Whom! ...Shall we the strong, strong defend?
Pack of dog...down the street...truly we saw!!

Sleep on Kerneelsie, sleep long...
We'll keep this fort, with song!!
Three blind mice...no trice...NO! IT's a FROGGGG!!
Wait! Waaaiiit! It could also...demmit...be a doggg??

I wonder, really by my thunder?
Just...really, really maybe no-one knows?
Weather all us cats...and all them dogs goes...
Heaven all our own...still, still wonder by thunder!!

There must, must be ball and string...
Bird or two...no! Lots of wing...
Mouse like us that never, never die...
And Darn cats in the sky that fly?

So!! Kerneelsie sharpen so long that old claw...
THE WHOLE BOXOMDICE...WE'LL SHOW THEM MORE!!!

by Dawid Brink
© pic Jorandey

MAR the WARRIOR

Mar breakout in Praise and song!
Raise, Raise like nothing is wrong...
A Sketchy hand in the sand
On paper black and white your photo stand.

Blood-washed he'll withstand the foe?
Power heart, hand foot and toe...
His heart sturdily wild and strong!
To his Master he, he waited long.

His saving story all does know...
Battle to blood his enemy wow!

Precious seeds out of love He sow!
From the mighty Spirit it flow!

Young and strong... yet, yet he goes...
Where serpent evil, only Father knows...
Over, over land and sea... Spirit He blows!
Power of Jesus' Love on him grows!!

by Dawid Brink
© pic Mar

STAR~LITE

With fluttering tint...magic everywhere...
Tell me! Tell me, who painted your hair?
Sparkle of silver, sparkle of lite...
Strong in spirit...strong in fight!!

Your romantic heart to steer...
To distant shores, none to fear?
Graceful thy countenance...
Courage grow...all mountainance!!

A Saviour your tender heart adore...
Praises!!! To Him you will roar!
Star and moon they too adore?
All in power and grace, from your core!!!

Sleep soft, sleep lite...sleep tite...
My Love...x...don't let them bloody bugs bite!!! LoL!

by Dawid Brink © pic Star

WHERE SHALL WE GO?

O! Where! O! Where shall we go?
Where no-one, nooo ooone! ...know!
Like the wind we ride, ride...
Gallop...gallop full in stride

Do you know...
Where the sweetest grass grow?
Wildly...under hoof poundin blows...
Green, green I know this meadow...

Our mane flying up in the wind...
Racing...you in-front, I in the hind..
Over mud and stone...
Yes! Yes!! We have flown!!!

The day full of eats and to play
You abide...thus, thus me to stay!! Aah...huumm!!

by Dawid Brink © pic Mariette

THE FINAL MEETING

How my heart was really achin...
For how , how long I've been waitin?
All my nights have slurred away...
For you my love...stay to stay??

The beauty of your steady brow...
I'm! I'm! So, so ready, ready now!!
My dress is Righteous You...
My heart and inner-core, I do!!!

Take me in your arms strong and sure..
No! No! Need for enticing lure...
You my heart of hearts I found!!
Now! Forever, ever You and me are bound!!!
Love me to rest lay, lay on Your chest??
Final, final at my very last only...past...to rest!!!

by Dawid Brink © pic Silvia

SUNSET STORM

Storm in my heart, storm on my life's sea...
She...She's all, all precious to me!!
Tempest toiling winds...raging waves...
You my love...me from life-billows saves??

Steady, steady...now, now my heart!
No! No! She's my love not to part!!
Grow faith, hope and NeverNeverLand love...
She'll soar...gentle back like a dove?

Deeper life's end, my heart to fend...
Golden Glow, Pumping low...you'll mend!
My regret strongest still...
Repent, repent my love I will!!!
a Calmer world sea...calmer heart of heart..
Never, never me and you'll part!!!

by Dawid Brink ©

The Battle is real.

Rest.

Rejuvenate.

KINGDOM FIGHT

O! Lord!! Indeed to You I bring...
Your praises...praises loudly we'll sing!!!
Kingdom Yours...greatly, mightily unfold!
Strong in power, love and bold!

Daniel's statue...big and tall, down You crumble..
satan's all forces brought down to humble!
Thou O! Lord's Church in stature louder grow!!
dragon hoards...bring down right and low!!!

Jaron!! The Lord surround the strong with song...

Millions...millions bring in all the crowd!
Praises! Praises!! Shout out loud!!!
Honor and Glory! ...Him to honor!!
Under satan's bonds no, no longer!!
Bring, bring heaven's host all, all along stronger!!!

His army marches very, very strong and bold!
All kings and princes...they all have been told!!
Leave out sin, stand long and hold!!!
Till glorious call...gathered in His fold!!!!

In Jesus Name...by the Blood we claim!!!
From Father...by the Spirit...Glory, glory NAME!!!

by Dawid Brink © pic Bowman

THE KING IS RISEN!!!

The KING of kings..He, He is risen!!!
Out of...out of death's prison!!
The key of death and hell..
To you I, yes I do, do compel!

Victory of victories He, He is won!!!
Raised IS..! Raised IS..! God's only Son!!!
The Holy Spirit He, He gave Him Life...
To purchase you and me His as a Wife??

The seal, seal death's tomb broken!
Yes He indeed...He made it open!
Death sting for us He gave a token..?
Holy Spirit!!! Yes! Yes! We have awoken!!

The holy angels praise sing!!
Let all...all heaven and earth glories ring!!!

His Holy Kingdom You have raise!
Michael won! The Blood won...the Son! Bring Praise!!!

For You O! Father! He'd bring!!
satan's defeatin bow! Praise You my Glory King!!!

by Dawid Brink © picture Carol

COME with ME

Ring ring O! my soul aloud!
Two's is a pare...Three is a crowd...
Will you sing to Him a praise?
He will save you...just be amaze

Lift your voice...you have no choice...
Heart heart-deep will stir your voice...
Bubble up...Spirit out your dept will flow!
Rivers unstoppable in Power will grow!!

Him adore you do...restore thy life...
He will give to thee thy wife!
So praise Him...stop the strife!
My love greater than your "Universe"...deeper than oceans
deepest life!!!

I ride wilder horses in the wind!!
Mountain skipping… all the way you will laugh..
Your soul to the highest plane...I will draft??

by Dawid Brink © picture by Lizette

FATHER of GLORY

O Father of Glory, tell me again Thy story?
Of Your great and wondrous Love...
Painted across the stary sky above...
Glorious worlds You have presented bold!
Yet not a tiny tip is now still unfold!!

Where do You go when Your heart is sore?
When sin Your people still adore?
Push...push You O! Mighty God away!
A million armies to slay...
Who holds Thy hand...death's play??

O! EL ELYON! of Power, Love and wrath?

Who's soul willing Thou wilt longingly hath??
ALL! But ALL! Through My heaven display...
Alive! Alive! In bliss forever all must stay!!!

ALAS! ALAS!! Alas!!! Send I My Son to die...
His Glorious Blood paint My horror sky...
Therefore men and women in this race...
SET! SET! Your heart to ME at pace!!!

Glory! GLory!! GLOry!!! GLORy!!!! GLORY!!!!! I! I! Will Show!
To me... Him stretch to me, strong and low!!!

by Dawid Brink
© photo Dawid

REPENTANCE of a KING!

O! Sin so deadly and foal!
Makes Thy sinner in agony despair deeply howl...
Where O! God...do I so far away hide??
Thrusting my spear deeper in Thy side!!

O! My soul deepest, deepest sorrow's regret!!!
Have I peace cast away...just simply...to let??
Shudder my being through agony!! I will...
Still...thrusting my spear deeper, deeper still??

O! Saviour wash with redeeming Thy Blood???
This dark stain...clean from slimyyy muuuud!!
Fair, Fair O! my Lord!...clutch You I will??
Clutch my cruel spear-hand I still...

O! Thrust my bleeding heart!
With Thy soothing sword...to start...

Words...Sword-words, Your' Masterly-art!!
Redeeming Love...Healingly bring Your part...

O! So glad, glad my deep, deeper inner being!
That I would ever enter longingly seeing??
THY THRONE GLORIOUS DISPLAYED??
IN THY LOVING ARMS...THERE...SNUG...TO BE LAYED!!!

by Dawid Brink
© picture Benjamin

INSPIRATION
The GREATEST MAN in History!!!

HE had no servants... yet... they called HIM MASTER!

HE had no degree... yet... they called HIM TEACHER!

HE had no medicine... yet... they called HIM the HEALER

HE had no army... yet... kings FEARED HIM!

HE won no military battles... yet HE CONQUERED the WORLD!

HE committed no crime..yet..they CHRUCIFIED HIM!

HE was buried in a tomb... yet... HE! LIVES!! TODAY!!!

JESUS of Nazareth... SON of the MOST HIGH... EL ELYON!!!

© Jennifer Powell
SOLDIERS for CHRIST
© photo Rebecca Gonzalez

HOPE ENDS WHEN YOU STOP BELIEVING

HOPE in HOPE

Watch your flickering light...flicker of my life
Doubt and some dispare...your only wife?
Hope in HOPE...my only Hope!!
Slippery slide...slippery slope??

Who shall anew direct my slippery path??
Lead me, lead me...just to laugh!
Show me, me show you...my only love?
Treat me, I treat you...gentle as a dove...

Cherish me, I cherish you...my royal Prince...
Your gentle look...Your gentle touch...
Your approval, my heart longed very much!!

Hope in The only Hope...Your my desperate HOPE!!!
Slippery lives...slippery mouths?
Do take motes from thine eye?
Displace despair...new HOPE from lies...

The room lit bright... from YOUR FLICKERING LIGHT

Light...so, so...bright!!!
by Dawid Brink © ...

HARVEST TIME

Over lands He roars...fields are ripe...
Bring in the rows, He roars...bring in very tight!
Golden shine the Live giving Son...
To Him dear, dear soul do run...

Lion...Lion of Judah strong and fair.
Sing a song, a song wild will declare.
Harvest Time, time is over...
You and me in His grip...be ye sober...

Sing aloud, very loud sing...HE DIP IN BLOOD!!!
POUNDING WHITE HOOVES MAKE HIS BANNER FLY!
OH! OH! OH! why will my fairest die?
TO HIM WE FLY...TO MEET MY BELOVED...IN THE SKY!!!

by Dawid Brink
© photo by Chrystal

LION of JUDA! LAMB of GOD!

The LION....OR....The LAMB?
WHO, WHO before you will stand??
Conquer your soul...HE WILL!
Soft like GOD's LAMB HE's still!

ROAR!...ROAR! Mighty victory roar...
my KING...my KING I...I ADORE!!!
The LAMB...GOD's LAMB...HOLY BLOOD HE POUR...
mine, mine yesss...mine is Heavens door!!!

ROAR! ROAR! ROAR! The UNIVERSE TORE..!!!!
THE LAMB...GOD's LAMB was drained...
From HIS BLOOD...THE CROSS was stained...

Runs, runs into the sand...in ALL of the lands...for me He was maimed!!!!!!!

DEEP DEATH CRY...depth of hell is shake

I T..I S...FIINNISSHHED!...AAAH!

The whole earth VIOLENTLY QUAKE..

The Lamb...Lamb of God..

Blood...HIS Blood...HE presented...DOES satisfies FATHER GOD!!!

by Dawid Brink
© photo D.C.

FRESH FRAGRANCES

Tint in a seductive bottle of blue
Red array out your exquisite flair
You a fragrance breath- takingly true
Curly soft tumble down showers of your hair

Darting aromas of you tease...float on a breeze
Graceful elegance 'forever' in blue jeans
Curvy ecstatic grip me in a tease...
Eyes sparkle dazzling with life...it seems?

Gorgeous etch images of you smuggle in my head
Bubbly personality...who dare keep a lid on you!!
Kissable lips...man ye have to be fast...it's said...

Bundle of Fun with you in a dance...I'll think it through
Orchard blossoms is in your eternities that will last

Two handsome hunks...and ...Rissa the rose
Fruit from that sexy stunning body
Yes! Life surprisingly here also dealt its blows
Triumphantly await soulmate eternally share thy Lobby...

by Dawid Brink © pic Ursula

ON TOP TILL DEATH?

You so damn 'shining' and 'bright…'
Rule in iron on top…you…with all might
Morning till night you sat on me…firstly so light
Harder…harder…till subsided I… without a heavenly fight

O! Your exquisite beauti bedazzle me
Beguiled…stripped clear of my manhood…see!
Who could fight this in-toxic lovely death…
Sucking out all my, my last breath…

Many a men…by the millions they all…fall
The happy go lucky…fat…even the strong, the tall
Jezebel's… Delila's… still their stature on…grow
Let's catch them…mall them..with our toe

Sucked dry on my bed finally I lay
'YOU WANT ME ON TOP?'...YOU SAY...'
Your walker right on my throat...she me slay
I in death 'controlled state' will I at last stay...LOL..

by Dawid Brink
© pic Naas

For in Jesus Christ neither circumcision availeth any thing,
nor uncircumcision, but faith which worketh by love.

NEVER! EVER! BE DERAILED!

Faith and Love feed on our Heavenly Dove
Send from a Loving Father and our Lord above...
Sure this Law of Life runs like on iron rail
Will deliver all the 'GOODS'...without fail!

With all Power you'll be endowed from on high
To remove lies, sickness...evils spirits that rob our sky
If our loving obedience firmly stand
We bring Jesus' enemies right down...grand!

But...O! O! Alas! UN-forgiveness forever rule
Derail your Glory Gospel train from rail in duel
Everlasting Father will keep you in His debt too!!!
Embrace your grudges, to you...it stick them like glue

Forgiveness releases you from own desperate jail
Put the Glory Train back on rail...not at all THAT frail
Damages that rip and scar are made undone
My forgiveness was won by... the Blood of the Son!!!

by Dawid Brink © pic Rebecca

MONO MOTION

I.....give.....you.....devour
This...is...turnin...sour?
YOU NEED' BE SHARP!
T'MORROW?... PLAYIN HARP?

One...thing...I...did not...see
That...that...would...it be...me
Mom has surely not told?
SON, DO FIT IN BOLD!!

Guzzled up...bit... by bit... in love?
Disposable... looking up above
Yet write a word clear!
No! No! Not a tiny bit of fear...

by Dawid Brink
© pic Marinus

AMAZING RYS

We fondly off from plys to plys
WoW! Caught in the Amazin rys
Awesome rapt in bobwire and lys
Cheers & sneers dazzle smeers my fys

Gorged out valleys in bliss
Soarin miles high in cosy thermal
Heart has skipped a beat, nestle up near a-miss
Forgin me in grace eternal

Bro and a Sis all Bloodwashed!!!
Transformed into…Magnificence!!!
Resurrected madly Loved
Royal Priestly standin in His Presence

Final Destination everlastin nirvana

Till then sweat, joy blood and tears
Protection all around Hosanna! Hosanna!!
Joy unspeakable to calm smoothly our fears

Sharp call to you friend of mine!!
JESUS CALLS! PLEASE COME AND DINE!!!

by Dawid Brink © pic Marinus

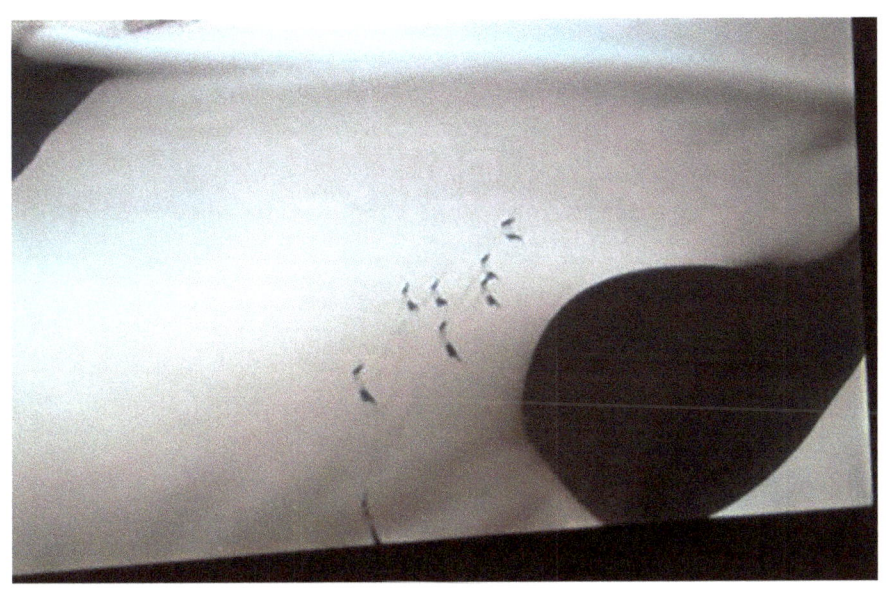

DESERT SPLENDOR

Stunning display across vast flaxen sandy blanket
Gemsbok magnificence survivors in the harsh
Dauntlessly dusty dunes expanse a ready hatchet
Magnetic invitational splendor quiet grainy-death marsh

Monotonous earth stretch of charming virtuoso fatality
Indifferent silence of your murky kernel millions
Stinking rich in nothingness gripped in seemingly immobility
Sand-curtained feet hang and roll suffocating granule billions

Many' a caravan you have wholly devoured in sandy glaze
Innumerable brave a warrior digested in thy bowels

Parched skeletons protruding bleached white in a scorching blaze

Untraceable magical…Fabulous treasure…clutching by a hole

Pebble-like specs of amazing animal splendor

Dry desert illusionists fascinating lovely creatures

Beguiling noble pompt to us be render

SIN HAS LEFT IT's DAUNTING STAIN…IN GOD's UNIVERSE IT had FEATURED…

by Dawid Brink © pic Discovery TV

TRANQUIL LURE

Wrapped in a twisty waxyyy haze…
Blooming flower...a rose...yes me stand amaze
Sun-rays playful, up and down magically appear
Cloud in mountain merging back in a rear
I...standing breathless in awe with no fear

O Valley your misty vapour, indecisively hang low
Lush forest growth caught through splendor...we know…
Morning and dusk day by day explode...then implode
My blurred vision expanse in massive over-load
Leaves me ecstatic floating in tranquil mode

Prompt me...a connoisseur of sight, sound and colour
All my vibrant senses, mindless afloat in valour
Scenes of mediocre life displays sometimes in mist

Rolling out endless scrupulous set-outs of a list
Entangle me in a void of fight with fist

HUSH! HUSH!! hush!!! All looks perfectly all to well
Dose lazily unaware off to a sure, sure HELL!

by Dawid Brink
© pic Mady

TRIUMPHANT ON THE WAY

The horses are gathering, jump lousy bail
'You're the head and sure not the tail'
Someone powerful and strong...yet not frail!!
Left satan's magicians and witches stuntly pale

In the Name of Jesus demons flee
Come you dirty hoards we cut your slimy cords
Blood of the Lamb powerful-overcoming cover me
Shield of faith and God's word piercing swords

Victory Royal Crown He Kingly worn
Key of death and Hades has He from satan torn
Living in the eternity of eternities
FEAR NOT! Rest on me! I carried your vile infirmities.

Glorious victory song raised, Sing out loud
His conquering banner fly a white horse through the sky
His enemies subdued, all the foul old crowd
We hooves all thunder ride along! My! O! My!

Dawid Brink © pic Sanet

GOD's CHAMP of CHAMPS

Some of us are...crooked...broken and marred
Cruel blows theirs...we think we knows
But 'CHAMPS' RISE UP THOUGH BATTERED and SCARED
Life dealt us down and dark enemies fleeing from us they goes

'FIGHT THÈ GOOD FIGHT of FAITH'
God's Champ lay down dead in the ring
St Paul...wounded, bloody broken by stone...made angels sing
Beaten by whip and stick YET! He rises in Jesus SAFE!!

Be it her life, looks timid and so frail
her body pure a spirit'll stay...like an angel she sail
'CHAMP of CHAMS' sweet Linandi do hail
Treasured more than gold in her we hold

Three medals of gold...record broken...of old
Champ's chip of St Paul's block in Jesus' fold
Faith strong in Jesus..He promised nothing'll go wrong
She glide on glitter air then break out in song!

by Dawid Brink © pic Zyna

BOLD COMFORT!

Bold, comfort she may find anywhere...
I'd push out her own, in danger to roam
Occupy I the wing, and wolves sweet, for her to care
How could I've known...reap what you've sown?

Brooding over me with so much pride
Her chick squeakily moans its frail cover blown
From my world sacredly I'll hide
Away my mother've thrown Kentucky breast and wing on loan

What an oddly doddly trio we make
Cuddly chrippy chicky could've flown, catch the tone
Right to your heart...Triple we do take
Wrapped snugly in cone she's in other zone

Beware where woolly warmly you, do abide
Chicken breast or wing may not, protect from his swing
Cute as it may, look does it, even by the book
Your world as it's known, would be abruptly shook

by Dawid Brink © pic Josè

SPOTS

Snow-leopard beauti rosetted, thy spot
Fury Ounce-pelt she's snug and warm
Playful stuck out mighty a paw

Mark over all your smell, pin your plot
Eyes no fear shown teeth in a growl, laugh at a storm
Rocks and Snow peaks and fresh icicles...I saw...

Tread she light stalking a prey, it'll escape her not
Blends in perfect each dark spot I'd sworn some dot
'Survival of the fittest' still our nature's law

You maybe stealthily my friend, I got...
'Leopard's don't change it's spots'...I mourn...
'Would you change?' at my gut it gnaw...

by Dawid Brink
© pic Lizzi

82

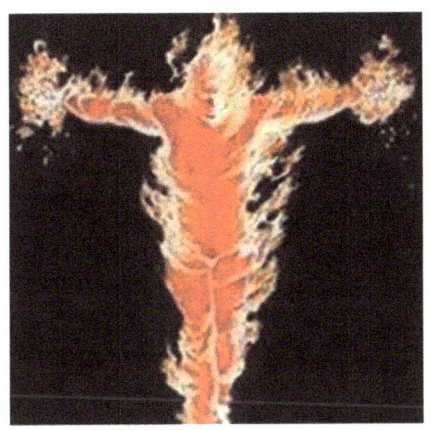

CLEANSING FIRE

Soul in Holy Fire..
Seek way to cleansing
Let your Flame grow higher!!
Purify thy heart...be sensing

Power... a Holy Flame
Heart to heart, bond thè relationship
All flee in Jesus Name!!
Rulers of darkness they'll loosen and flip

Heart with truth alined
Flaming Sword exceedingly sharp
Cut and shape our mind
Joy only our song...sweetly on a harp

Shield of Faith flying arrow...dead it stop!

Saving sandles score a soul on board
Vanquishing Victor, satan's hoards we rob
Flame forged to YaHuSHua Ha' MASHIACH...HIM I adore!

by Dawid Brink
© pic Cindy/Rose

RIDE of my LIFE

Ride with me Love
Hair flyin in the wind
Lovely exquisite my dove
Laughter echo...I in the hind

Hooves of power underneath it pound
Your cheeks rosy bunched in a smile
Layin lusty low in saddle we go round
Racin, racin the wind...it's been a while

Our hair on end up around the bend
Leather...Laughter...Loud...a shriek! Hangin on a cloud
Our heart poundin...mud the hooves up does send
Hi! Ha! Hi! Ha! I love you...shout...I...loud!!

by Dawid Brink
© pic Lana

LADY! LADY!

Lady! Lady! ...of high stature and pure class
Picture... Pretty...Poised...flower through crystal glass
All arranged, exquisite colour displayed...in a vase

Lines softly around your sweetly array
No-one really knows high price you did pay?
ALL IS WELL! ...I..can tell..what do you say?
Thorough-bred Yeah! ...both body and soul
Yes! Yes! ...even Jesus made me whole!

Business Guru and in hard of life
You have been such a gorgeous wife
All fair blond bubbling and bold, just a little…strife

Through hardness...brute-world you'd go
Tirelessly trade...love and weep...what you sow?
Jesus came when you bowed low...down...low

by Dawid Brink
© pic Belinda van Loon

BABY in a TREE

Baby in hiding splashin it, it be?
Crooked, twisted floatin Laughin in a tree
Picasso drawn? Wow! Freak of nature there stand Sue &
Shawn
Under thè hangin tree, just set for me

Find I the baby none, my life thrown from
Tree touch two hands stretched out...see?
For us a dream...painted...please set it free?
Universe of water break, birth me to take...

Pregnant, promise, prevail eternally not for sale!
Standin on a sea-shore...new beginin we adore
Cuddly soft in burstin joy we'd pray before...
Once it's there we say: Please, It's not fair!

Dirty nappies...puke...foal it has brought…
Really, really take it away this I not sought
Friend! Joys, toys and little boys all you caught...
The day you'd pray...Yes! So let...the...baby...Stay!!

by Dawid Brink
© pic Status of the Day

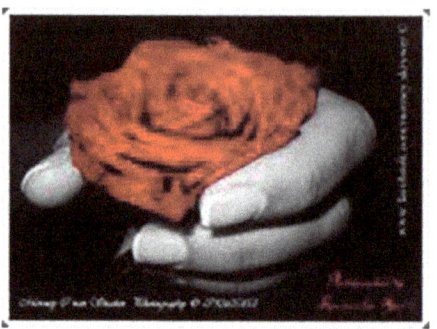

54)' MAN O! INSPIRATION...

Breaker! Breaker 4! 24 wheeler roar...
Hi Buddy, what have you in store?
A Poem of beauti and some sound advice
Get those Guys...back there, the drivin lice!

It's a long, long windin road
Soul tire'in, through the black lint unfold
Diesel and dust...end of the road I must
This old load dispatched in towers of rust

As crimson horizon lower down to dusk
Jesus, me and 24 wheels deep I trust...
Breaker! Breaker 4! Morney give me more!!
Encouragement....somethin..to...chew on...raw...

Windin roads of intrigue's of life
Cheer and gladness...death and so much strife?
Ah! Make it worth...awaitin my lovely wife
Friend's INPIRIN WORDS...BREAKER 4...O! Rose of LIFE...

by Dawid Brink
© pic Morney vStd

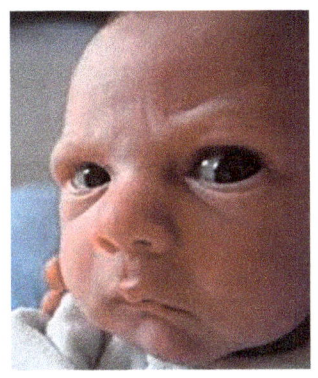

WHO ARE YOU…?

I really didn't want out!
No...need! No...need to shout!
Just...who, who are you?
I'll throw at you...a shoe...

Could you be a God?
A Mom...or a...Dad so sad..
Or...should you be a God?
All the world you know's pretttty mad!

Think I still, still must longer hide
While you...yes you! My aarrrival abide?
Unless you can prove…otherwise…
I'll...I'll give you one! Howzat for size?

So...? Leave me in there alone...
Comfort so and snugly a zone!

by Dawid Brink
© pic Aurora

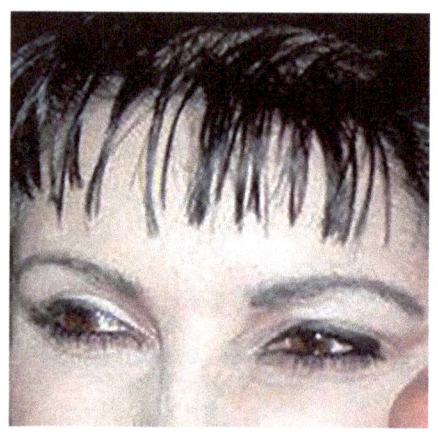

LOVE THOSE EYES

True beauti within..love those eyes
Smilin Yeah! No...No lies...
Openin soul O Windows...what pleasant surprise
Pure spirit...heart when in love...surmise...

Praises us a Poets, thinks we'd all know'it!
She blumin smart...lovely...she'd shown it
Chatch'em them devils she goes a trapp'in
Truthy machin thrashin...up, up joys She's lapp'in

How gorgeous intriguing in these eyes' been
Words out a pen flowin character and beauti seen
Poet pulse'in in bloom...fills heart n soul
Romantic, then pitch black moment deep down...mole

Eyes of love Thankful above
Hardship's I've had
Made me...black and sad
Yet! one look...at...you
Amazin what I've been through
Does never leave me blue...
Swell, celebrate life Yahoo!

by Dawid Brink
© pic Lizette.

MIST...A REACHIN...

Mist...a NeverNever reachin silhouette...
Empty a arm, stretchin NeverNever I get?
Holdin in mine embrace thee NeverNever let?

Teasin your lips...rosy fleetin mine it brush...
Explodin to my brain exquisite the...rush!
Just to pull back, my...fingers...not...a...touch...

O! How...I long to hold thy face...
Wrap thy gorgeous frame in velvet and lace...
Just...to slip thee...out...at my place...

Soft thy hair fall flowy a wave...
Deep, deep in my heart you'd cave
In memory...in-bedded thou stunnin layeth...

In quiet...stillness O! breath of night...
Fleetin a memory...you...in flickerin candle light
Heart's achin, longin for your warm embrace

Spread out stary host...sparklin bright...through the night

by Dawid Brink (Hanlie Leach)
© pic Lisa

INDJUN & WE

Popcorn and beer
Indjun! Wat'ch ye rear!
Ha! From we not'th to fear!
We'v all systems in gear...

Snoopy dog and pals
Wha'ch got that sells
Burger'a fries..oil o' wells
On Thanksgivin 'non' she tells'

Tis' them day alll be well
T'moro out breaks ALL of hell!
So! Me pals lets celebrate!
T'moro Politacy lock' our gate

by Dawid Brink
© pic Rhonda

LOVE dreamy LOVE

As I hold you, you so dam close
Hear the beat bounce of my heart I suppose
Touch light my face...tippy touch my heart
Excited I adore you, clingin...never apart

Your muscular frame coarse against mine
Eternally in bliss I'm sublimely...all thine
Unlockin thy intrigue mine
Inner-soul song reverb so fine

Dreamily on sand I lay
Quiet waters in ripples play
Mould thought of you in clay
Crimson sunset in you hair... touch... I if I may

Deep... deep... my love for you
Never... never... this partin, if when this is through
Please dreamworld... please... wouldn't you stay
'The Promise' eternal be you! Yet! Another day...

by Dawid Brink
© pic Classic Love Songs Danila

HEART OF A LION!

Young lion, Lion Kami's ROAR!!
His enemies shudder and shrink down more
On praises 'LION of JUDAH's likeness you soar...
Bold, Fearless in battle...that the Spirit was given for...

Nicol, Pinki, Anjum, Julie Christine Anne and me
Inspiration for Mashiach's...Young lion, yes! We see!
Born anew your heart...never you 'd turn and flee
LORD GOD for Mount Zion FIGHT, I sides Thee…

Wound by buffalo...open it tore...yes we saw!
Yet! Once it's healed...on it's back dive once more
Danger in his face...not retreat one pace
Jesus be my Star! With Him Victories won by far!!!

by Dawid Brink
© pic Kamran

ADAM & ME

Adam: Halve of my halve… was so easy
Father formed me dust and clay… sleazy?
While asleep deep my side…I didn't peep
Eve my love… down fall… did He weep?

Me: Entire Universe stunnin a beaut, I'm to choose
Sue, Pam, Bridgette, Con Riana…who would I loose?
TO MANY! TO PREFER… MAKE MY HEAD SPIN…AS TO BOOZE
Be it her…Royalty the like…THE WHO's of WHOS?

Adam: Yes Lord she the only, only one
Camel, Lioness, Tigress… Hippo I shunned
Snake wow! Giraffe…Orang-utan I 'runned'

Had it easy son, yet I would've been 'funned'

Me: Hit a Miss... Hit a Missss, Has, hasss it come all to thisssss?
LoL! What a glorious game to play?
But let Father decide... who should stay??

by Dawid Brink
© pic Ann

HEADLINES..OF MY WORLD

Refreshing my cup, spread I glass over eye
Reading me...start I...before 'me' my now world fly
Page one, over my paper, eyes run...what? Why?
News flash all today, .greet I, with a sigh

Bad news...Good news...my world shout
Tear me down, build me up strong sometime other weak
What does my world's paper, boom news to you
Would you joy or cry when I'm through

Page to critique column...read me good and sad, get mad!
Classic's page...my heart broken...still for sale!
Comic strip...ha! HA! Brighten my life through
Business column...friends, shares they have bought

Enjoy sports page, games I played... won some and lost
Injury reported...contests sorely missed...
When life's final race be run ,THE CUP won!
My paper be it file 13 or displayed where all have shone?

by Dawid Brink
© pic Susan

PASSION is YOU

Touch against thy chin…my lips do…brush
Soft silky my hand on thy hair send forth a rush
Thine eye tells stories intricately in dept…thy soul
May I unlock strings of joy from thee leapin like a foal

Exquisite love let me draw laughter from thee
Skin of velvet rapturous tingle me through and through
a Tast of thy kissable lips of rosy
Let me hold thee snug and cosy

10,000 kisses will never leave me satiate
Warmth of thy touch in I do gravitate
Worlds of wondrous…no escaping bliss

Gorgeously, fearfully fabulous thy lushes I'll miss

Intertwine inseparable thine heart receiveth mine
Intoxicating bubbly flow to my head thy wine
Float us away through pearly marsh-mellow sky
Passionate love, creamy chocolate floats round fly

Kaleidoscope bungee Turkish-Delite velvet feeling
Implode exuberant our worlds together void a sealing!

by Dawid Brink
© pic Ann

DESPAIR to LIGHT

Lost, lost is all?...my rage turned to despair?
Greedy tricksters evil hoards, stripped me bare!
My soul is raw, eyes dry...is there any who really care?
Have I received my due? Mine what is fair?

My home be at loss! At What, what a cost?
Despair can like thick darkness grow..
Became for me? 'Reap what...you sow'?
Is? ... IS? ... this, thisss where I'm brought low?

Red Crimson tide...does spell out with my LORD awesome ride
JESUS has flooded my world, deep in my soul HE preside!
Streams of Blood like these, me…HE has washed me whole!
Even long before 2000 years...spirit, body...and...soul!!!

Utter despair...birth in me new opportunity of LIGHT!
By You O! Spirit of Love and Power, teach me to FIGHT!!!

by Dawid Brink ©

WHO! Is WHO?

Who! is Who! You!… You...and You?
A Sheep goes bleat and cow goes moooeee
But You! ...is you and I am me...
You got them feathers, I got them fleee...

My world...I eat them bird and mice
Two a duckling I eat trice
Yellow and fluffy, my cheek will be stuffy
If ? ...liiii...eat... and devour thee, am I Scruffy?

Innocence of...of beauti rare
Life turn out, out not so fair
Survival bring out THE BEAST in us
Tear at each other grow on ugly...Yea!...like puss

So...while in peace we may, can fluff and fir…??
Tillll fierce old dragon up, up we do stir??

by Dawid Brink
© pic Michelle Laas

O! LIGHT...LIGHTHOUSE of GOD!!

Battered by mighty rogue a wave
Through storms deep they cave
Many, many a men thus has been save
Be it sun or rain it does do slave

AHOY! AHOY!! The warnin shout!
Steer to stern...THEN...TO PORT!
Soul in despair, out it brought...
Hope of dear life desperately sought...

Beacon...O! BEACON of hope
Flash thy Light...sound thy Warn!
May it be Peter...may it be Paul...afloat
Thrashed by life and people' scorn

Yes! Men of God have gone before
Stood weary, strong the test of time

Warnin, Pleadin...Boomin their roar!!!
Standing on 'THE ROCK' O! O! STAND SO TALL!!

AHOY! AHOY!! AHOY!!! JESUS SAVES!!!!
AHOY! AHOY!! AHOY!!! COME!!!! JESUS SAVES!!!!

by Dawid Brink
© pic Carol

BOY! O! BOY!

Boy! O! Boy!...YES I reeaally would!
Yet! I don't know if I should?
Bust his eye...yes! He lies!
LET HIM COME! To me...if he tries!

Boy! O! Boy! Bring my train and toys...
I'm mad...yet! ...it makes me sad
Determined to get my own
Hey! You! Give back what you've loan

Boy! O! Boy! He don't know it yet...
I like and love him...friends for life we're set...
Mine is he...friends till...she...
Sera kissed both him and me!

Boy! O! Boy! Does Jesus see?
My love for Him and thee?
Grandma I'll get them and me
Sera and he, to NeverNeverLand we flee!

by Dawid Brink,
© pic Jorandey

Color of your purse should match your dress

COLOR OF OUR PURSE? Vs COLOR's OF OUR HEARTS??

From all walks of life...we toil and strife
Caring purses big and small, some single...or a wife's
Matchin my dress...matchin my shoe
Paradin world's stages of...who is who?

Yellow, red, black...crimson...brown...even green
Presentin precious belongings Ha! Not been seen
Pressed down with bags like this in the heart
Weighted on wheel each day, weary we start...

Boxes? Purses like these, fill mornin till noon
Yea! Yea!! will get rid of it very, very soon!
But what will we gape about, who will we swoon

On who will I dump my filth and thrash under your moon

My color MATCH!! But here's the catch!!!
It's grown in size, what beast inside will...latch?
Consume me...no matter he will rise!
Cheer UP! Little Lady!! Sit up! NOW BE WISE!!!

There is really some-one so very Fair...
'Come to Me'...'Your burden Please? I do, do care...'
'Dump it ON ME...EVEN YOUR FAIR SHARE
ALL THE WORLD's FILTH I DID, DID MYSELF, FOR YOU DID BARE!!'

by Dawid Brink
© pic Giel

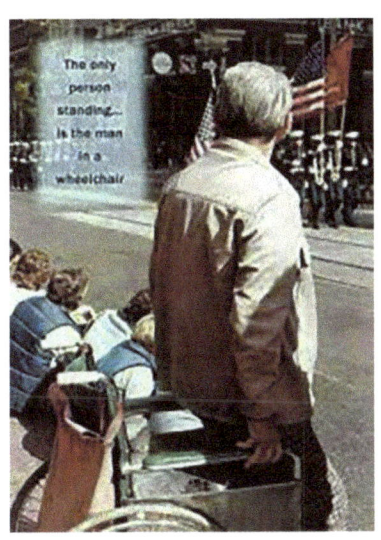

WHEELCHAIR PALS

Me and you on the streets of life
You am got some sticks...I got some wife
I've been lonely, your wheel's on the run
I ain't got feet...us...to feel and have fun

You see me..., I see you...
Men without hope and lame
Your legs of clay, mine in Life's game
They all sit...and may I stand UP to fame?

Minds eyes retrace our steps
Yours... stumble and shake
Mine... humble souls...it may break

In time with joy... I may awake

At last rays of hope lit brightly through
You...was I...! I was you...!
Mine a chair...I...was alone...standing up
The Likes of you sat, while I'm through!!

by Dawid Brink © pic

WOMAN OF WORTH...RIANA

O! Life to you have dealt deathly it's blows...
But bravely you ride his storms...it shows
No corner or, or 'CHECK MATE' to you does it holds...
Or..lol...can cast you...ha!ha! In simple moulds...

Your boldly...lovely...honest smile of pain...
Stronger, stronger Jesus' Power you gain...
Eyes...eternal depth pools of raw passions...
Million of year...load...flay down in sassions...

Eight...make you in anguish...helplessly cry...
Eight...rolls, rolls almost make you die!
Eight...glorious eternity, number His Name...
Eight, eight joys Ruaan...sparkle my flame!

If ever I hold you close drain your sorrows in flame

Close hold, suck out your pain, what would be my gain
Jubilant bubblin hearts that's not vain
Forever embraced locked in blessin reign

You are so much substantial, heart filled in Love
Beauty exquisite...Love...Gentle...as a dove

by Dawid Brink
© pic Riana

CHRISTIAN SOLDIERS FORWARD!!!

Fierce rage the bloody battle, scary the cattle
Blazin fire and brimstone porin wrath
'SWORD OF THE LORD AND OF GIDEON'
War cry shatter the silence...breakin forth!

Sword held high...in crimson sky
Shield brace strong, arrows long
Lion's claws sharp, teeth bare!
Judah's Champion growl and roar!!!

Be courageous...heads to be protected
From blows attacking our glorious salvation
Word of Truth split wide spirit and soul
Demons flee as soldier's legions roll

LIFT JESUS HIGHER! LIFT JESUS HIGHER!!
His Blood claim victory time after time
Love poured out!! Praises we shout!!!

by Dawid Brink
© pic Rebecca

PAKISTAN FOR JESUS

Our heart of hearts in deep agony...we cry!
Don't let, let our people, people in their vile sin die
Urdu...Punjabi...all tall, small...handsome and fair
Your Peace...Victory...Bloody battled scared, we care

Every inch of land, lofty mountain high, across all our sky...
Deep wide over rivers, in dark caves..Your message fly
On wings Angels...Eagles the like, the gospel drives it's spikes
With love conquer hearts of parent-less child...over mics
'COME YE HEAVY LADEN...AT JESUS' FEET LET YOUR BURDENS
DOWN!!'
He'll forgive you… washed in His Blood...even give you a
crown..

Heed the SPIRIT'S CALL Paki's WHY will you in ALL eternity die
You could be with Jesus forever changed...to meet Him in the sky!!!

by Dawid Brink
pic Pakistan for Jesus ©

OLDER I GET

'at the end of the day, all you can hope for is to go on. The older I get, the more I realize that just keep going on, is what Life's all about! ' .. LiesL MarX

At the end of my day...
There is...a more...excellent way...
HIGHER and HIGHER
To climb with JOY! in my step
I tell you...stay

At the end of her day...
Is there a more excellent way?
Still...Higher, Higher...Still
Do climb with JOY! in her step..
Yes! A more excellent way!
I plead you...do...stay!!

At the end of our day!
We found a more excellent way!

Soaring Higher, Higher fly?
Jolt of air...caught our wing
Stay...the UP DRAFT...Stay!!!

by Dawid Brink
© pic LiesL

SAN's DONKEY RIDE

Brown her donkey, dark her glass...did he run?
Through chalk whites, whites bleachin in afternoon sun
Dazzlin smile, auburn hair tumblin...straddled flair...
Happy as lark...your face with glee spark...free of care

Black your cheerily array shapely leg across donkey spray
White his unwilling mates, some saddled master in wait...
San ecstatic, jubilant she rides on a trot, smile a mile wide...
Much so much enjoyment laughter...fun...lazily they run!

To-night in fleeting delight she may wonder, yet... she might-
Two Angels flicker through, momentarily her mind toss
A wish...a sigh, would their hair of locks in wind lightly fly...

Their laughter tingles her ear, flashes aches of pain her hear?

Pregnant Mary mother of Jesus...jolt up in her mind
Astride donkey, belly swollen anxious...place, would they find?
Triumphant Jesus on foal of donkey, Jerusalem streets He tread
Vividly strikin her mind, mind of Messiah..where He did Bled..

Hosanna! Hosanna!! Rings in her mind, eerily loud!
Branch of Palm greet Ha' MASHIACH...hearts of stone, men so proud..
She ponder...ponder glorious thoughts... so profound..
Smiles bouncingly, break across her face...left her astound...
KING of kings they bear insignificant me, on their backs here are found!!!

by Dawid Brink
© pic San

HIS STRIPES 39 X

Thirty...Nine...Times...Nine!
Stripes on my Saviour's back
Flesh ripped out, Thirty Nine Times' of whip O! nine
NOT A WORD DRAWN FROM HIS LIP, EVEN...SWINE!

His Face drenched in a Bloodied mess
Spit and Blood mingled, drippin down...
His Beard clutched, ripped by fists of clown...
Torn to shreds in heart, later they confess...

THIRTY...NINE...TIMES...NINE
'Let us feast...BRING THE WINE!
'king of the jews'...yes was His sign
Bore ALL FOUL SIN...YES even mine?

Marred more than any, any man...
Stripes of shame, bring healing to us it can!
Eco through ALL TIME..those LASHES WILL CHIME
For meee!! NINE...TIMES...THIRTY...NINE!!!

by Dawid Brink
© pic ThirtyNine Times

SUNRISE JOY!!!

'Sunrise brings Joy of Life as the Pages turn a Leaf in Living in the Moment of Time...Mwah!!'...Cindy/Rose

Joy of Life the exuberance of my soul...
The Journal of Life flipped yet another page...
Openin a new curtain of Moment on Life's stage...
Life like a rose burst open, birthing me whole!

Moments hung in suspense, us greetin the sun
Like a champion awake, his Life just begun
Crimson glare over waters, cheerful my stare
Golden glow of warmth, breaking my sky so fair

Glimpses of Moments in time...ecstatic, make my life rime
Alive with fragrance everywhere, mixed with...
Rain and dewdrops, bird flight's high and swift
Pulsating Life's Glow explore, my world of Thine

by Dawid Brink ©

LION OF JUDAH

O! Lion, Lion of Judah long...long you've roam...
Far North to South...West from East...to Rome...
Killed...slaughtered...spread like dirty foam...
On waves miles high, high...as from earth to sky

Jerusalem beloved holy city, city of our God...
Blood drenched your streets...even...Messiah Son of God!!
Lifting us to Royalty...Bride...Eternal city, city of God...
Jerusalem, Jerusalem we cry...Yes! Yes!! Therefore He did die...

O! O! Lion, Lion of Judah...Eternal King of kings
Our love, adoration and worship gladly brings
Let us soar up! up! To You...Power currents on wings
All the world He saves...All Israel, Israel wave on wave

Gentile marked line, O Israel now's your time

Rise...rise O Judah, Ephraim...brave soldiers of Mine
Battle...battle cry...the Sword of the Lord and Gideon
Be strong...the battle's the Lord's all...all along!!!

Trust Him Him alone O! Israel forsaken, forsaken so long
YaHuSHua Ha' MASHIACH! LION of JUDA restore your ISRAEL-
SONG!!!

by Dawid Brink
© pic Ify

SECURE in BLOOM

Bud perfectly splendorous...sublime immaculate line
Petals...each one's array Unmitigated impeccable mine
Glory flawlessly...nearly...velvet His hand formed thine
Each velvet-silk securely in glass, fragile so fine

Your bloom open...burst of `color bloody your red
Earthy raw fixed in your stages flaring wide so it's said
Imagine thy fragrance rupture exactly a petal in my head
Lock in glass, till public display planted in flower bed

Mysteriously exquisite grace thy velvet's hold
Fragile thy aroma would tease men wild of fame and bold

Balanced in glass, suspended in time...breakable ahead...just fine

O! How precious thy wait...rewarded like matured wine

by Dawid Brink ©

CRIMSON SKY

Amber-fire...bliss aglow...crimson flare...
We shot the sky with paint, paint so rare...
No painter...painter could really, really match
His canvas much exquisite my breath do catch...

Lazily elongated in bloom setting sun...a silhouette...
Outline shapes I become... strokes of black and palm
Stretched out sticks, splash against burnt sienna sky
Suspended across in space-high... my heart fly

Orange delight, delight in snug warm embrace..
Drowsy flutter your beauti-face..I swathe in fine lace
Playful lapping wave...spatter softly on stretch sand
Ochre...peach brush amber-smear over dreamy island..

Misty tangerine spray...moist tipped my nose
Watery arms of foam...grab at my tight buns...those?
Stars will glittery soon display...splashy appear
You in my arms holding...quiverin body...no fear

by Dawid Brink © pic Alwena

79) UNIVERSAL DISTANCE..I WANT TO KNOW YOU!!

(Matt 16:15-28; Rev1:5-18; Eph 1:15-23)

O! Lord...GOD!! EL ELYON on High!!!
Saviour of my sinking damned world...I'll fly!
Up! Up!! Up!!! Through cloud-crimson sky...
Color my Universe...all my why...Yes! Yes! Why..?
Prostrate before Thy glowing pierced feet...still...I lie...

Love, love to know Your glory face all the more...
Cleansing Blood washed.. all..see you'd have in store
Nailed to that agony tree...in...me, all..tenderly You bore!!
Death slue 'old man' You drew...lustful desire...You wore

Open heart's eyes, all Thy treasures...Thee to adore!!
Spirit of understanding and wisdom all before...

Anointed resurrection, Mega Power...O! Death we arise!
Raise the dead..Jesus said..Thy enemies we despise!

Thy golden see-through heart...I want to YOU be treasure
Only! Practice Thy precious Presence now...my only measure
Love to know Thee! Love to know Thee know me, that' how I'll
grow!!!

by Dawid Brink © pic Lizette

FIERCE and RESPECTFUL

CATWOW-MEN! Fierce stare...findin thee is rare...
I'm now your track...aloud desperate your prayer...
Speed, agility and strength you wow'nt escape...
Maybeee! If your cunnin...stealth...yet might evade?

Somalian plains my Queenly form does be graced...
Two...and...four...yes! Be our swifty legs...is it waist??
Proud Royaly our heads firmly held up high!!
Lean...muscularly tough...bodies, race against sky

We're perfectly matched...defend...attack with might!
Our territory stolen?...buttt we'll not give up her fight
Children happily adorn our lairs...in jubilation a bright light!!
Preserving beauti-grace...extinguished from sight!!!

Owe it all sweet Saviour...creation's stunnin world!!
Sacrifice all, all Himself this universe, He'd be our wealth
Humbled respect each-other in awe restore our health
O! Heart a Soul surrendered in full flight...my world!!!

In Glory He cruelly died savin souls under Somalian beauti sky
Amazin, mystery eternally...reveals all in time...of just...why??

by Dawid Brink
© pic Alwena

TATTERED...I WILL RISE!!!

Frail...frail my beauti, my beauty...also torn..
My glory array so scared...so scared..I'm worn..
TELL ME! All forlorn...for this, why I was born?
Cat battered...chilled wet through...by storm

Head pretty now, now you go...hung all low?
My life...life I, I hate...hate you so!
Treat me bad! Treat me lo! On, on you go!
Why, why in life's despairs tantrums me, you throw..

Angel wings be clipped...wings, yet they grow...
To former glory steady, steady go a bit slow...

Friends me encourage...start my fire...coals a glow
Inside my core it stir...freedom juices flow...

His Holy Blood...life...red cleansin flood...
Savin me...plucked by friends from drownin in mud...

by Dawid Brink © pic Rosita

CAPTURED IN GLASS

Squashed down n glass...swallow whole...Yes all my soul
Wolves tear! You swear? Pulled open ...all ...is bear...
Raped my soul! Defiled my body, in his slimy lair!
Kill you! Burn you alive!! Humble you I swear!!!

Who shall take up...take up Powerful my flimsy plight
Stand bold Yes! Yes!! Yes!!!Take up now my fight!!!!
You'd strip my lip...shamed deep murky my inner being
With mine eye...blurry bloody...my heart not seeing

Stripped bear ...their honour...strip stark naked!!!
Expose broken core...No! No!!...so bloody sore!!!
Who gave you bloody right? Spills gut down's gore...
Desert dry...my eye did cry...desperate forsaketh???

Yet! Yet!! Will I rise...Yes!! I YEEESSS!!!...Will surely rise!!!
Beloved Maker, fearful wonderfully made alone in His eyes..
Mine tattered stature will grow...He'd all the world to show
Sure all in time...those tearin hoards..broads down all low..

by Dawid Brink ©

LOVE...HIS...ONLY...CRIME!!!

Death on a cross...HIS ONLY CRIME?
Love's utmost...just for me...dreck and slime...
Nail thrusts in hand, feet...and whip's bloody line...
You! O! Proud boastful soul, who's the swine?

Forgiveness!! His lips...Father...loud He plead
He'll be back, back riding ...riding white a steed!
What? What? Then O! Boastful soul you'll plead
Wipe your sin? In-vane, in-vane gush!...He'd bleed

Yet! Yet!! On rogue cross was He strung!
Drenched in agony...for you Jesus did hung!
Heavens choir His Praises! Praises Glories sung!
One soul in repentance...death's trap it sprung!

'I thirst'...so do you, you can satiated lie..
Alone...naked...'forsaken...My Father!' He did die...
ALONE...Last Holy breath LOUD, LOUD He did cry!!
'IT IS FINISHED' all hell jubilant God's Son'll fry...

His Crime of Love sends God's blessing from above
Broke wide...cleansing crimson's flow from His side
Grave, hell...death...sin...demons, none can hide!
Your foolish heart lost in sin...He'll grip in Love!!!

by Dawid Brink
© pic Annamaria

BREAD and POWER

Swallow, swallow bread to fill, wine... down it spill...
Nourish us still...feed you, make you strong it will...
Longing...Yes! Thirsting desire fatten thy belly still...
Urges, lust...crave deep, deep your yearnin and frill!!

Rise! Rise! Does bread only still strengthen thy power?
Will you draw, draw sweet victory only in that hour?
Ride a wave, brace a storm...smile at hurricanes warm?
Blow down tornado swirl...wasted breath it'll be... be warn!
YaHuSHua Ha' MASHIACH beckon...call...be fed, grow tall!

Word through prayer I'll eat...Body mine is torn...on you I feed
Gored... My Blood was drained...me nailed to that tree!!!

Cleansed be, with Holy Power...dazzle white purify Light...we shower

Draw! Draw...from Thy Bread... Power...unimaginable might
Raise the living dead...life...plunder the grave instead
Make Alive! Destroy demon holds! Strongholds sò bold
See HIM...heart's eye...look His face, you'll know why!!

He the Body-Head...living parts, build together a new start
Holy Spirit's flame, tongues and Power...spill...flood thy heart
Bread of Heaven feed through me...others, let it be?
Glory! Glory! So shall Thy Father...many sons He does see!!!

by Dawid Brink©

KOTIE's MURKY TRIUMPH

Sinking, sinking deep gloomy right down low
Down...down my feet in murky muddy water go...
Life-line in desperation please me you through
Piercing my heart...sorrow broke me down low I bow

Water... heeps of troubled waters of pain...just double
Piling up,up...piling every trouble, make me wobble
Bedazzled stupefied drowning sea of stubble
Satan's hordes rain and spill their slimey rubble

Unsteady feet shakily I became aware uncompromising
boulder
Growing staunch...unmistakable raises my head and shoulder
We never learn trust...trust until we much,much older

I CAN DO ALL, just expansive entire...wide in the universe ALL!

Christ Jesus rescued my soul...when my back's against a wall
Blood washed me, sin all erased...forgiven I stand tall
Washed with His word...lust, oldman, heart of stone...maul

Ransomed...He graced me!...
I'm free...open for all to see!!
No Water, nor fire-scourge...ever will flood ME!
Cause HE my Lord God, He'd with me be!!!

by Dawid Brink
© pic Kotie Brits

SILOUETTE...MICH

Reflection your silhouette...fondly play in my head...
Remembering the way, way you said
You're a 21 plus...plus flair in my blumin head

Who, who are you...you starin intensely through me
Piercin eyes...laughter play, play fleetin across your see
Smilin kissable mouth...luscious lips...for me...it be?

Fondly...fondly ponder...slowly...reflection in-bedded
Charmin gorgeously swim aimless through...my head!
Awake...awake sweet lady, you within my arms instead

Exquisite style...ravishing beauti...consumin thy fire..
Elevate my touch dimension still gloriously higher and higher
Disperse body elements...in planes..NeverNeverLand's
explosive attire!!!

by Dawid Brink
© pic Mich

LINE OF LIFE

Daring on life's line you go
Softly tread...on hard a track
Tail down straight your back
Steel..steel...steel hard lines flow...

Never meeting trotting...light fleeting
Two lines wide...boringly still the same
Mediocre...parallel's, no-one gets blame
None move away through rain or sleeting

Frail look your black spot
On a line with no danger lurking
You don't know if the train's working
Rumblin noise...run off your spot

Your lives are nine, only one...mine
My track is narrow...iron track is wide
Life is...the runaway train nowhere to hide
On the narrow...safely...my life is Thine

Click-a-dee-Clack! ...Click-a-dee-Clack!
Rails are sturdy, rails are strong
Glory train on and nothing go wrong
You conquer all and cover my back
Click-a -dee-Clack! Click-a-dee-Clack!

by Dawid Brink
© pic Lizzie

UP! UP!! MY WORSHIP!

As...as I lay prostrate before...Thy Throne...
In absolute awe...awe Thy beautiful Stone...
Come I in total worship to You all alone...
My God! My God!! I in despair do groan!

Open, open my blinded heart's eyes
May I see Your Face before I die
In heaven's view...hollow depth...my souls cry
For me!! ...Yes for me!!! You did die...just...why?

Lamb of God up, up my soul to You does fly
Hear my desperate cry...oldman you did die...
Accept, accept my frail worship on high!
So in my last ditch...before Your Holy Throne I lie

Up! Up!! Our adoration worship arose..
Creatures...holy Angels,man...Elders...all of those

To Him Whom all Glory on High now belong!
Thankful proud we boast...Thy Blood...our only Song!!

by Dawid Brink
© pic Paris

WOMEN! ALL AGLOW!!
(Ezeg 36:25-27)

Women...fairer than fair...all aglow!
Thy inner, inner beauti...beauti...the world...thus show...
A heart wild...with wild-fire...passion go!!
Love seeds...sin's death...glory gospel...uplifted Son...know!

El Shaddai...righteous laws...Yes! My heart convict...
Sin's power...fouled my soul...it does constrict
Blood of Thy Cross...does clean my slate...sin evict
Spirit of God...deep inner being...fused in brick

Aglow! Holy-fire aglow!! Their heart pure...
Sin out...the old-girl...lust...is gone assure!
New spirit...heart of flesh...stone-heart out...His cure
Spirit we'd aglow...for sure ...world no longer lure...

Burst forth sisters, sisters in Glory...Praise!
Sow seed's...Power,Love..Self Control...yes! we says

We in victory, strongholds...satan's angels slays!
Hallelujah! Hallelujah!! Jesus we Praise!!!

by Dawid Brink
© pic Connie

WAIT!! ...WAIT ON GOD!!!
(Is 40:28~31)

Awesome...awesome power...of the strong, strong wild...
calming wind

Break apart paper, homes, forests, mighty ships...oceans rise...
blows our mind

Tornado's, hurricanes, monsoons...this breath of air bring rain...
cough up at will

Yet!!!...my Master tread on might roarin sea...ride boisterous
plumin cloud

Spit of YHWH's breath rush into formed dirt'...brought forth
Adam...out loud!!

Cruel cross...His final breath...blows refreshing burst of eternal
life...is born

Wind-breath of fire-tongue explode over satan, black
demons...down them He'd torn!

Millions! Millions!! Sucks this reviving fire-breath...new life then to
be worn

O! Breath that is God, blow in us explosive, vibrant life...that even raise the dead!

Feast on God's only Son...YaHuSHua Ha' MASHIACH...my Living Bread!

We will wait a patient wait for His revealing Presence...that we do once more...

Wing spread open wide...on Your Crimson Tide...through the storm may roar!

Higher and higher...till 3rd heaven in God's Throne room's golden floor...

Beautiful...frightening hurricane...Father's power in despairing hour!!!

O! Wind who is God...EL ELYON...raise,raise me a storm?

That I may soar on mighty wing...up,up to You...to where it's warm!!!

by Dawid Brink
© pic Silvia

You...a BRIDGE SILHOUETTE

You...my silhouette in hazy, lazy distance...
Are to me, a ever escaping,dodgy existence
Many a feet, coarse and fine...cross loathed bridge
Climb, climb high awesome,splendid ridge

You...my silhouette whom I ever...forever reaching
My hands in stance and strife...you yet breaching!
So near your silhouette bring anew me...a teaching
Yet so far, distant...how wil we be meeting??

You at me...do run...engage to have such glorious fun!
From hazy breaking dawn...till crimson setting sun
On a bridge out so far...on planks, none at all tarred...
Watery reflection images...her face riddled and marred

Eyes your exquisite soul-windows, sure could tell
Pain a loss...Heart of aches...where hard, you fell

Beautiful thy beauti face...wrapped all in exquisite lace
Convicted, stand in hog-like-dirt, could she...me embrace?

My dreams wrangled, draped...all wangled in a maize..
From lonely wry old ways...we're safe in HIS PLACE!!!

by Dawid Brink
© pic Lizette

LIGHT of my JOY

Love O! Love of my soul...
When, when will I be whole?
Riding a horse...riding a foal...
Love O! Lover of my own soul...

To you only you, to you I so do long...
For a 1,000 years I've been strong...
Heart of mine missing a beat, missing a song...
Lifeless and misery until you came along..

O! ...Light of total, total my joy...
Dooms and gloom's of us to be destroy...
I've waited, waited heart of hearts pounding...
For your Light of lights, that's astounding...

Dreaded night so finally, finally gone..
Joy...unspeakable your joy,you returned my song...
Heart of mine..for you beat very strong...
You...Light of my exuberant joy...to you I belong!!

by Dawid Brink
© pic Lizette

THE AGE OLD ARK

To NeverNeverLand...there we do happily all fly...
Through blue and thunder-cloud alike that paints our sky...
Sail on through might winds safe in my arms you do lye...
Singing praises to YaHuSHUA Ha' MASHIACH...

To starboard with precision our cannons flash...
Blasting arch-enemy with his hoards we clash...
Now to port blazing our sword and shield we them mash...
Through the ages battered and torn this old Ark goes on...
Driven by boisterous wind and hail and evil con...

This old church stagger strongly with power and might...
By the Blood of the Lamb we fight...
Our testimonials like toiling bells echo ...
Through Valley and mountain land, marshes and glittering
beach sand...

Ha' MASHIAH YaHuSHUA IS RISEN...
O YOU DEMON EVIL HOARDS...

JESUS MADE US KINGS, PRIESTS AND LORDS..
TRIUMPHANTLY HE GLIDE THIS OLD CHURCH THROUGH THE SKY...
SAFE BY THE SPIRIT TO JESUS AND FATHER TO A LAND WERE WE
NEVER DIE...

Heavens!! Glorious IS JESUS MY OWN LORD...
NEVER NEVER IN A MILLION YEARS COULD I AFFORD...
A PEARL SO PRECIOUS SO DIVINE SING WE WITH ONE
ACCORD...
MIGHTY, MIGHTY IS HE WITH WHITE HORSE, CROSS AND
SWORD...
COME ALL YE WHO DESPERATELY WILLS GO ON ABOARD...
WASHED IN HIS BLOOD FROM YOUR SINS BRIGHTEST, BRIGHTEST
OF WHITE...

FLEE FROM EVIL DRAGGING YOU DOWN FROM THE LIGHT...
YOUR ONLY PRAISING SONG, THIS OLD ARK MY ONLY VISION IN
SIGHT ...
JESUS Ha' MASHIACH LORD THROUGH ALL AGE OF TIME...
HIS PRAISES HONOUR IN OBEDIENCE ALL THINGS IN HIM RIME...

by Dawid Brink
© pic by Galina

A LIFE SILHOUETTE

Simmering dusk edged my frail awaiting silhouette
He...…Has…...His….mind on me...I bet
Has....His compelling lovely Spirit Toucccch you...mmm yet???
Only...in this aft...if you Him...will let!!!

My life with Him has been ever so glorious
Benoni...Sorrow-son, Benjamin...son-right-hand...
Mashiach Lord Jesus upon head of serpent He stand
O! O!! O!!! Astride white white fierce stallion His ride is
Victorious!!
Joyous vision flash vividly across my mind
Tender moments....lifting through sorrow a love so kind
Where did you waver off, rushing off...so blind??
Then O! sober-minded Lady slashed in heart, did she find...

O! Glorious out off the fire like she was snatched
Blood of the Lamb and THE NAME..NONE MATCHED!!!
Unsearchable..ever was such Power be found!!!!
LOVE ENDURED!! To HIM everlastingly is bound!!!!

AWESOME!!!

By Dawid Brink
© Pic Jeanine

VICTORIOUSLY I FLY
(Rev10:7 against Eph 3:10-21)

O Gracious Lord my God on High!!!
Graceful on wings of a dove I fly
Through clouds mountain tops go by
Exquisite flutter my heart my body edged in a cross...O why??

Angelic hosts and demons hoards attentive hear!!
Jesus Lord Mashiach and EL ELYON made the master plan....
Forever!!! no-one here would ever fear!!!
His mystery many sided-wisdom, to you...I can

HEAR YE!! O HEAR YE!!! Principalities and powers we to you
disclose
His Master design unitedly save Israel and Goium
He satan's and fallen angels trix wide open did expose
Holy Bride...my outstretched arm to hold Him wholesum

Enigma mystery of mysteries for ages to man and angel closed
O AWESOME FATHER Your Throne beckons open wide
No enemy low can block His Crimson Tide
You, in horror held hostage, twitch...where would you hide
His Wife flooded and filled with God Himself
Experience His Utmost Love in abundant Wealth

By Dawid Brink
© Pic by Cherian

FEARLESS IN THE ROUGH

Midst in twylight...at the set of sun
Tired of the exausting breaking run
His life he'd scarsly won
Wild river..Stag-boy he'd shun

Dying sun last lick'off old mountain range
Turnin his head ..think it's strange?
Silhouetted sticker-arms stands a tree
Yes! Yes!! He ran himself right free!!!

Sworn enemy in the haze...
Ball of fire ..yet ablaze..
Blinded his vision of what he saw
Fooled....like us in awe...

Bushy shrub like water flow

Safely hide the Stag inside
Roarin!!!...it looked wide..
at least it's attack it brought to a low

by Dawid Brink
© pic Wilmien

A LIGHT…A BRIDGE…A RIVER

A Light breaks through as dusk settles a heart
shearin heavens fractions apart
burstin through dark rollin cloud
Piercin …warmin the mountain high

Revealin in its ray magnificent old bridge…invitin to cross
Pillars sturdy, stout solid they on rock unmovablely stand
Strechin across great divide…which many a wheel toss
Safe beautiful even kingly the curvy line

Ragin even stormy powerful chrushin waters flow
Neath glorious bow of strength, protectin glory train
Windin over rock and stone curvin danger grow
Rushin on destruction path, down over valleys below

Such picture give me risin growin hope
When in darkness we aimless grope
There is 'THE LIGHT' who shows 'THE BRIDGE OF WAY'
IN WARMTH SUNLIGHT SNUGLY WE CAN STAY

ALAS!! LET LIVIN WATER CLEANSE YOUR SOUL
SPIRIT BODY AND TO OTHERS FREELY FLOW!!

by Dawid Brink
© pic Wilmien

MY WEBSITE

I..l.li..Weave my website of lies and deceit
Trapping weary man to utter defeat
Thread so very deceivingly fine and amazingly strong
None...none of you would be wiser...none is wrong

So you say:'Come out to rough and play'
Itsi bitsi spider catch me if you can!!
See! If I easily break through your silky fan
Of tangy sticky tread...left me to stray

Cunning and schrood...yet...so inviting
You stick gripped tight to it like lightning
How many hits do my website have and mountable?
To millions no billions no! I bet uncountable

Catchy dragnet of sin and woe..
Each will reap only what he sow
Only Only the BLOOD OF THE LAMB
BREAK FETTERS TO PIECES...JUST GRAND...

by Dawid Brink

A TENDER TOUCH

As...as...I...hold..your precious heart in my hand
Glowing in the warmth of it I stand
A shudder crashes through my soul
O! O!! Alas! How...do I keep it whole

Delicate O! O!! So soft my quivering touch
As pure as my array...sparkling white..and much
I in wonderment and in awe I just stare
My glorious gift amazin from you so, so rare

If I ever so squeeze it real hard it could die
But....if I really, really cherish it, it will fly!
With me to NeverNeverLand through the starry sky
In bliss forever on puffy clouds we will lie

by Dawid Brink, © pic Alex

REFRESHING FLOOD

When we down to nothing
God's up to glorious something
He Powerful with love reigns on high
Wings like eagles takes you to the sky

Living Water seems to be wasted
If but you o sinner have tasted
Awesome water so deep refreshing
This Water and His Blood a blessing

Where in the desert of sin will my thirsty soul
Be rested...revived and made completely whole
Tested and tried in a furnace, battered faith
Down at His feet I myself now doth lay'th

Glorious streams life giving Waters flow
His precious Blood cleanesth, Thy Spirit make me glow
Powerhouse grow in my inner being
Gushes forth free to all now be seeing

Washed, I'm clean by Your Word
Banished my idols with Thy Blood
Created a clean heart in me O! Lord!
New is my spirit pure deep within
O! Stony heart all, all broken apart
Rise o willing soft flesh heart of mine
Powerful Love O! Spirit flooding my being!
(Ezeg36:25-27)

by Dawid Brink
© pic Carry... & quote 'when we down to nothing. God is up-to something'

THE BATTLE GOES ON

Darkness verses THE LIGHT
Ages to ages on goes the fight
Some-days easy, at times..with might
Morning noon and night

Never in fantasy may we live
A head...a hand...
where do you stand?
This battle is real so is the strife

Victory of victories had He won
Golgotha's cross...and...the tomb
Our sin? Nowhere to run? To Him we can run!!
New birth we be birthed from heavens womb

Our powerful weapons are not carnal...see
No enemy before Thee may stand to prosper...
principalities and master spirits before us flee
Strongholds we cast down...all them are foster

The BLOOD WILL PREVAIL!!!
To JESUS our LORD PRAISES we HAIL!!!

by Dawid Brink
© pic Lonnie

YOU AND MY SUN

If I could grab hold of your Sun?
And not have me on the run
Just imagine the world's we'd won
Casting great balls of fire...so much fun

Nourishing, bathing warm, soaking up water for a storm
Charging up and stimulatin growth
Dis-banning cold and darkness of form
If I could swear, I would... swear an oath

Sun-ray bring vibrant living life
Over thistle thorn, labour and strife
Ripens the harvest and all delicious your fruit
Glorious flower and all things good

Master...MASTER of the SUN!
It is You Who has won!!!

To You we'd run!
Get all the Sun and even lots of fun!!

by Dawid Brink
© pic Paris

BEST FRIENDS

We're like David and Jonathan..
Through thick and thin we'd been
Kings and paupers all we've seen
In creep deceivers..hoard's of satan

We stick closer than brothers
Our lives offered up! We'd give our all!!
You more dear and precious than all others
Against all fiery onslaught we stand tall

Our blood allegiance firm it stand
Your family like their blood is mine!
Where ever we are and you need a helping hand
To the rescue till death my body on the line!

Once not so many moons ago
The Son of Man died alone for His friends

On a cruel cross, their and our sin His life He did throw
To His Father reconcile them...us, He made amends

Friends The Lord Jesus calls us!
Best of the very Best!!! Why the fuss?

by Dawid Brink ©

TRADE OFF's

When last we're all spend
Curled up...no-where to be warm
I've traveled to worlds-end
Not a single shelter from life storms

The 'Trade Off' thing we can do
Worthy stuff exchange hand to hand
Some will be glad some will be blue
When bargains are through...who will stand

Friend the price of Love
Is ALL OF YOU AND MORE....
Glowing befitting tight like a glove
All you can muster....ALL YOU HAVE IN STORE!!!

There is 'THE ONE'...we all have shun?
Taught us the 'TRADE OFF's'
of LOVE is UNCONDITIONAL?

by Dawid Brink
© pic Kerry

ALONE...

Us alone...a friendship word
Against alone...a devastatin word
With Him alone...a comefortin word
Alone...a educational word
Alone...a restoration word
Alone...a isolation word
Alone...a revelation word
Alone...a searchin word
Alone...a dreamy word
Alone...a cryin word
Alone...a passionate word
Alone...a close word
Alone...a punishin word
Alone...a bliss word
Alone... a selfish word
Alone...a intimate word
Alone...a exclusion word
Alone...a painful word
Alone...a powerful word
ALONE...a JESUS WORD!

He...brought into this world
He...tempted
He...on the mountain...
He...with the Father...
He...with His disciples...
He...with Talita Komi..
He...with Lazarus..
He..with a unbelieving crowd
He...with the harlot writing in the sand
He...in Gethsemane...
He...with the mockin soldier…
He...in Gethsemane...
He...carried His cross...
He...on Golgotha...
HE...MY FATHER, MY FATHER…
He...in the grave…
He...with the keys of death and hell!!
He...faced demon hoards
He...He gloriously risen...
He...in the room with...Thomas...
HE...WITH OUR FATHER
HE...WITH YOU!
HE….WITH ME!!!

by Dawid Brink
© pic Paris

THE HUNT

Dangerous sharp my horn, powerful...neck and long
Agile pouncy a step on hoof firm my tred
Taunty tough my hide...patients my sure abide...
Death claw on my back be...may this my final song

Bulging a muscle, dust swirling thick beneath claw
This way and that...masterly her plan of attack
Fierce primitive a battle I ever saw
Three deadliest on a quest
1 afore 2 grace my back

Beautiful life is a battle underpin love and strife
Stoically aware, race a 1,000 options on the go
Dance-duel with awesome death and life
Head down low striking a heavy blow

Thoroughly meticulously plot each-others downfall
Some slain victim...that leave a bleeding conquer
The excitement of the hunt Raise a call
Salute beauti and gori-one must fall that's the story

In awesome life...we...win or lose
The battleground is for you to choose...

by Dawid Brink
© Painting.. Heléne Kapp Artist

BETRAYED OUR YOUNG???

Thousands of young boys shivering...grave scared
Living dead...they plod on
Their lives ruined to death...and...marred
Hey laddie! I have colour cladded candy...so sad?

Let me be-feel your strong boy-body
'fathers in cloak' boy muscles I must have
Come in my 'holy office' I'll lay sin-hand on you
Lustful eyes ravish young flesh...nervously he laugh

Tears rollin rivers and cries of pain
Cringed in fear... heart broken... in... shame
'father, father...tell me...this...ain't sin?

As he pulled up his fly...right there! I could die
Millions a death death down on me it rained
Confessional box...son...there victories are won...

Tom, Dick and Harry! Join me in the vestry... famed

Convicted for so horrible foal deeds done..
Bright American boys...played...as...toys
Grey-suites coldly except bribes...maybe my son?
pope bless leads to bishop and cardinal robes...for their ploys

Many a young-one take the eternal plunge
In icy rivers their bodies coldly float
Next year these vile grey-coats grace our podiums...
RAISE UP A STANDARD...AGAINST THEM...ENOUGH is ENOUGH!!!

by Dawid Brink
© pic Lily

OOPs!!!

Yes! OOPs! I've done it once again!
There? There is no end to the pain...
My wadin big mouth and soarin foolish pride
You can tell me nothin careful things you've hide

Those...those treasures you did motherly pamper
For a fool like me it means nothin but thrash and mud
These make you shrink in agony and in hidin you'd scamper
Plasterin it splash! over the net for every stud...

Is nothin pure and sacred...holy anymore?
Slashin hearts, eat them alive...apart yes! we tore
No matter if my words my dearest friend is flayed
Tramplin carelessly their trust aside sprawlin it layed

by Dawid Brink
© pic Luciana

LOVE'S INTERTWINE...YOU AND I....

Glitterin eye...sparkle with starlite-dust....Thou!
Brightest of brightness my sun-world ...Thou!!
Rainbow kaleidoscope of colour-array explode my sky...my
Exquisitely Thou!!!

My sun-world is pitch-black ...an endless snakepit...
without Thee?

Mistical, tropical...Forrest -mist of smell thy hair...Thou!
Earthly-fresh with sea-sky smiles....My Thou!!
Tender maiden's purity thy adorningly form ...
My   Exquisitely Thou!!

A snake-slime pit...pitch-black my sun-world...without Thee??
Thy lark singin, my sweet singin...Thy feelin, my eternal
contentment...Thou!
Thy sincerity...my constant tranquility...

thy presence, science of my home...My Thou !!

Thy slim hand, are my rough hands...thy excitin step...

my ever safe pass...My Exquisitely Thou!!!

Understanding-heart...happiness-heart compliment thy flawless character draw...Thou!

Passion-wine's immaculateness of taste...your life's adventure my only reason...My Thou!!

Intoxicated bliss that super abound bountiful...

My Exquisiitely Thou!!!

Sun-world blackout...snake pit...lost without Thee???

Thy feather-light steps, my impregnable path...

velvet thy skin, how snuggely I wear...Thouest!

Thy bleach purity most brilliant, prefect sparkling diamond...

My Thouest!!

Eternal precious treasure...

Mine Fantastically Exquisitely Thouest!!!

My....scourched...sun-world death-blackness...Shatter my pregnant world of ultimate expectation...LOST WITHOUT THEE????

Thy vivid exploding dreams, mine ...

Thy rervealin presence...my joyest jjoy...Thouest!

Thy absolute, total surrender...Thy heart O!!! my Queen!!!,

my final arrived destination...

Mine Only Thouest!!

Thy succulent lips, my flower-honey...

Thy silhouette breakin dawn...my

Exquisitely Only Theest!!!

Thy deeply understanding me...
as blissful beach to golden sand...Thouest!
Thy high and low understanding...as
Sky mountains, as to abysses depths
of eternities...My Only, Only Thouest!!
Experiencin Thee as giant like tree, embalmin beauty flower...
My Fabulously Exquisitely Thouest!!!

Thou supportith me...as powerful song to extra-ordinary singer...
Joint breath...inseparable,...as sea and beach...
Intertwined...as step to foot Print...
As time...clock and clearest chime...
As virile fish, in sparklin pond...
As cool refreshin breeze, a top misty heat...
Thou art blissful smile on my Face...
Thou art life-givin water that satiatin my excruciatin thirst...
Missin Thee
To esquire Thy expressive presence...

Blackest nights of nights...Thy absence...
Black! Black!! Black!!!
My sun-world evaporatin...
Black hole of endless nothinness????

Eureka my!! Discovereth...me Thou, right before me...abrisk!!
Thou my only achin need, understood my deepest innercore
being!!

Embracin tranquil love, comprehensible tenderness...
vigorous, vibrant
Sincderity from Thee my lovely dove...
I'm Thy upliftin wind...Thou art soarin eagle!

I'm Thy very pulusatin heart...Thou art deep-innercore being!

I'm pitch black/dark/pale night...

Thou art glisterin, romantic moonlite!

I'm blazin consumin fire...Thou art ever eternalburnin log!

I'm radient bright your sun-world ...Thou art my dancin ray-lite!

I'm crashin, ragin, destructive sea waves...

Thouart my dancin frothy,

Playful wavetop foam!

I'm your resoundin clear echo...

Thou art my expressive boomin word!

I'm most incredible journey...

Thou art final destination!

I'm dark mysterious excitement...

Thou art explosive exuberant light!

I'm volcanic boomin eruption...

Thou art blazin crimson magna fire!

I'm forever windin twistin road...

Thou art beautiful fullest holdin way!

Thou art coolin shady tree...I'm dark mysterious forrest!

Thou art refreshin pourin rain-droplit...

I'm brightest lightin flash-lit!

Thou art rock-solid reason...I'm crystal bright pure motive!

Thou art unwaverin clear sound conscience...I'm explicit exposin science!

Thou art anticipatin pregnant hope...

I'm humblin bold confidence!

Thou art erruptin bubblin fountain...'m estatic lovin holdin way!

Thou art glitterin crystal-line glass...

I'm tongue spree sparklin wine!

Thou art ecstatic beloved...I'm tender embracin love!

Thou art magic golden sand...I'm majestic awesome Everest!

Thou art flare dressin array...I'm crowned glorious head!

Thou art stunnin amazin picturesque gal...

I'm expressive glowin eye!

Thou completely satisfied my ragin thirst...

Thou rock-fastly support my spinnin world...

Thou lavishness overwhelm me as none ever would...

Thou abducteth stealthily me to exotic NefverNeverLand....

Thy scalpel, delicately...fearfully...

tenderly flare my lovin heart like a

master surgeon...

You're the broadest smile, on my kissable lips!

You possess the liver-tender love of my heart!

You comprehend me in quietest of silence also ragin babblin
speech!

I'm decision...Thou art strong will...

I'm 1,000 sunsets...

Thou art 10,000 freshly graced, blissful sunrises!

I'm majestic effort...Thou art mighty movin ocean!

I'm very alert attention...Thou art crisp... sharp decision!

Thou art perfect, still peace...I'm boomin order!

Thou art unwaiverin faith...I'm deepest passionate love!

Thou art ragin battle...I'm fearless courage!

Thou art graceful fingers...I'm iron-strong hand!

You patiently and passionately feed me,
when I'm totally famished!
When I'm chilled to bone...
your warmth embrace...heateth me!
Thou give me drink, if I thirst!
You add to me, lavished passion, to my incredible adventure!

I'm your enchantin melody...Thou art my reverberatin,
perfectly intune Guitar...
I'm your revitalizin dream...
Thou art my kaleidoscope of fantacy!

You're the only cure to my tortured affliction...
You're my pupils in my eyes...
You're my extreme excitin voice...
Disbannin harsh, desert-desertion, loneliness...
You're my hopes hope, my inspiration exceedingly to excel...

I'm THY CONSENTIN SACRIFICE...YOU'RE MY CONUMIN ALTAR!!!!
MY LOVERLY, ONLY LOVE and LAUGHTER IN MY SOUL!!

By Dawid Brink:
© Reworked from Connie's LOVE...YOU & I

PART II: Afrikaans POEMS WITH UNIQUE PICTURES

VLAKTES van HOOP

Kaal lê die vlaktes oop
Skoon my wêreld gestroop
Ma weet jy daar is nog hoop?

Laat son, kleur oranje in
Waters blou...sonder fin
Wie sal jou ander rykdom gun?

Nuwe hoop, vlaktes lê oop
Water plant saad in hoop
Jy sal nog nu plan benoop?

Bruisend onderaards gebrul
Hoop vlam op, hart...is stil
Weet net HY STERK die Wil

deur Dawid Brink
© prentjie Sanet/Liz

KOTTELJONS

Dans,dans my Kotteljons!
Jou litte los, die riele gons
Lyf van jou...di ruk en rol
Nog al, da by di 'Mall'

Wi sal wiet wa di Gangtag lê?
en Wat sal djou mama ssê?
Wiet djy wa Emma da le?
Of? Dans...djy skapi me?

Wi kin djou hart si pein...'there'?
Djou se voet di drai tot hane'se krai...
Rrriele lllyf...va di wjin ssstoook stjifff...

Hi djy! Wiet djy...vanni Meestir se plan?
Dja? djy wi di spies, an Sy, Sy an?
Grot, grot moes Hy ly!
Da djjjyy vylig in Sy arms ma vly!!!
deur Dawid Brink ©

MY SIEL is OPGEHOOP!

My siel is geheel en al op...opgehoop...
Deur...deur die gange van die dood...
Waar het, het jy te lank en ver geloop?
Deur strate reise van siele dood...
Is daar...daar nog steeds hoop?

Hoe het jy so...so verwronge, verward, verstrengel??
Gegryp deur n valse geslepe 'demon' engel...
Ja vasgegryp...baie stewig geslyp!
Maal kolke, dool howe van vergetelheid...

Vergrepe vas, vas...so vas gedrepe...
Gestrand...ja verlate gestrande skepe...
Altyd op reis na verre, verre lande reis...
Na 'mis-mirage' NeverNeverLand se hys!

n Liggi da ver, ver my rede 'hocus focus'.
My laaste riel...veg hard die dode-kus!
Lig in lig word die gange mooi...

In goud, pêrel, diamant wit en rooi!!

Duistenis maak stok, stok, stapel blind!
Niemand dìt dan rerrig ooit kan vind??

deur Dawid Brink
© prentjie Alta

STRALE VROU

Afgeëts jou möie strale krans...
Röi glinster...jou hare in n dans!
Wit jou prag lyne, slanke lyf.
Gedruk jou hand teen bene styf...

Skugter röie möie lippe lag!
Wie sou jou broosheid op wag?
Blik...sagkens neer gevlei...
Arms en lyf...prentjie möi gelei...

Jou stralelyne skitter stanz gemaak?
Kuiltjies diepe...aksent jou gelaat.
Wie sou jou skoonheid, ooit ontluikend laat praat?
Skitter-wit, jou hals möi te laat...

Veruklik möi jou ëts getöi...
Glorikrans van Hom aan jou gegee...
Bring vreugde-vrug so mee...
Duisend...ja duisende maak ander verleë?

Strale-Vrou ontvou...ek bring vir jou! Die son afgepluk!
Jou 'Universe' het ontvou! Möi...möi..Strale VROU!!

deur Dawid Brink
© foto Marietha Momberg

AMAZON 'QUEEN' van die LIMPOPO

Waar swaar, masjien krakend, breekend loop...
Jy Amazon 'Queen'...gedoop...Skeur die aarde rukkend oop...
Swaar, swaar masjiene het haar...haar hart deurloop...
Staal...gespierd klap haar sweep...in hart en wil...
Bereik sy haar pylge-ykte doel...rue sterk ma stil...

Diep...glinster, waar gulsig skatte pryk...
Rys...stof, swartdamme gemors en slyk...
Boer en dier word verja...ja verstar...verskrik...

Boom, plant, bos, klip, rand, berg, aarde oop uitgeruk!

Sy kyk n kyk wat Diepman's hartsnare ruk...
Wie, wie wil 'Queen' my kats kom...uitpluk...
Bevele...stratëe...bulder sag haar yssere wil...
Hel-laas...diè Baas en vergaderplaas doodstil...

Sprankel...mooi Opwinding...sy...haar prag gelaat...
Sou jy versoen sagvrou...lushof praal...
Haar liefdseun sy modder aard moeder haal?
Uit knarsslak steenkool...stankend swartdrek...
Limpopo 'QUEEN' Amazon sy reeds warrelend uithek!

Nog nuwf 'skalp'aan haar belt...kloof reeds aarde na nuwf
'scalp'..Sela

deur Dawid Brink
© foto Lizette

TUSSEN WOESTYN SPORE

JY...n senterpunt, in die nat...nat oseaan van stof.
Spoor na nêrens...nêrens lei...ja lei tog êrens.
Wyd...tot...Nou na jòu...dus, ja tog na êrens...

Jou...My deurmekaar wêreld dor, droooggg...bar!

Spore aangedryf deur gloei winde?
Reeds ook in my lank, lankal toe gewaai...en bar!

Sal dit weereens lewensaar voed..?
My...Jou?? wêreld bruisend ooop spoel?
Tot vrugbaar laafenend, borrelend oase...SY LEWENSLUS!!!

deur Dawid Brink
© foto Lizette

SPRANKELPOP

Sprankelpop...jy, jy met jou duet...
krulstert, pylstert...met vurk DIE het..
Dans met ysterskoene aan.
Daar...daar kraai die laaste haan!

Nakend voor het bebloed kruis...
Gestroop...helaas uit, uit Sy huis...
Wat het jou...jou tog besiel?
sy...sy laaaste daaanns jou, vi jou te riel?

Buite...JA!...BUITE staan jy met vlerk VERDWAAS??
Mar laat...laat...ttee laaat...heeeeel...HELAAS??
Jou...jou laaste, laaste dans SPRANKELPOP!!!
Jou plek, jou uit, uit die hemel lat HHHOOOP!!!

deur Dawid Brink
© foto Lizette

ZONKIND

n Vladder in my oog...
n Vladder in my hart...
Skuim op die sand...
Jou aan my hand...

Wind deur ons hare...
Lewenslus bruis in ons are...
Geroer diepste snare...
Oseane wil ek jou gee...
Dans op sand van die see...
Jou deurskyn wapper die wind....
Jy vryer dan my Zonskyn kind...
Zê my...Zê my...waar sal ik joue vind??

deur Dawid Brink
© pic Lizette

ZANY

Onvergeetlik jou oë
Smeul poel...
Ruk...gryp jy na bo!
Verswelg gevoel
Verlore in Hom...jy glo!

Klokhelder jou lag
Smeul poel...
Vreugdevol...jy wag...
Doelgerigte gewoel
Teleurstelling in daardie dag

Wa-wyd oop opreg jou hart
Smeul poel
Wie kyk verby...dai oë...sien die smart
Aanraking soel...

My kanse gesny na n kwart

Hare prag val in n krul
Smeul poel
Aan dai röi lippies smul
Jou vel koel
Avontuurlik ondernemend
los sy die spul

Gesofistikeerde aantreklike vrou
Wie dra jou op hande warm...ek sou wou!

deur Dawid Brink
© pic Lizelle

KRUIS, HAND en SAND

n Woord...pyn letters in die sand..
Geskryf deur, deur DIÈ Hand...!!
My...my boodskap voor mens en land...ja in die sand?

Net, net vir my te lees, sonder diepe vrees!
Ruk, ruk, ruk...hier...HIER BINNE my hart...
EN?? Hy, Hy kies...kies HY my, my se part?

Jy...ja... Jy ken, ken my smart...
Boor, geboor...deur, deur my hart...
Ek JA!!...JA ek!! SieleLiefling HOM't JY VERRAAI???
JA!JA! daar gaan, gaan die tweede kraai!!!
Verdomp!

Weer en weer...weer en weer, raak HY my...
Die Bloed stroom, stroom water en bloed uit SY sy..
Verswelg, verswelg is gans my wese...

Dit...Ja! Dit JA! word MY 'UNIVERSE'.......
Geheel, geheel my EIE LEUSE...DEUR MY EIE KEUSE!!!
deur

Dawid Brink
© foto Pancho Gepols... Morney

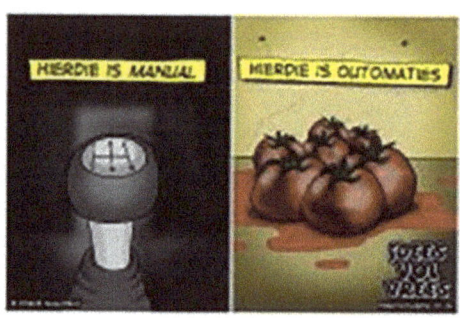

OUTAMATIES

Haal jy my uit rat
Agteruit veë ek als plat
My sin van die lewe
Rittelend...hortend bewe

Outamaties...vrot...verskyn
Brose mensies tog so klein
'Gooi hul in skag...Ja gooi hul in n myn!!'
Dan veg ek en jy...dis mos lekker pyn!!!

Outamaties is ek van my eer gestroop!
Waarom voel als net dood
Weet hul ons 'lieflinkies' het nood?
Outamaties dem lekka op brood

Kom sit ons stewig in rat
Kragtig klaar kloof ek die hout
Doelgerig peins ek die pad

'HET JY MURG IN JOU PYPE...
IS JY LAF of is jy SOUT???'

deur Dawid Brink
© pic Marinus

SPEEL, SPEEL op die SPOOR

Pappie, Pappie tog het ek jou lief
En jy is n monster JOU gruwel dief
Steel wreed heel my kinder lewe
Vry deur Liewe Jesus aan my gegewe

Alles rondom my word doof stil
Ook gedemp, gedemp my laaste gil
Word jy bevraag...skuif jy net aan jou bril
Sit ek tussen die spore, rammelend voel die grond tril

Yster spore koud van skuld en liefde
Loop wyd uit mekaar...doof-hoor...ek die trein
My liggaampie bewe seer, meer… my hartjie se pyn

Betraande oggies styf toe...ek sal nie sien hoe...

Knieggies styf bymekaar...pyn sal spoedig bedaar
Speel in my gedagtetjie...prewelend sien ek haar
Bebloed my moeder draai sy weg...of nog n vuis...proe!!

Liewe Jesus ek...ek weet Jy sal
My kom haal...nooit sal JY faal
Dreunend ruk die grond onder my...gedagtes maal
NOG n BROSE 'LIEFLING SNUITER' BEBLOED VAL.....

deur Dawid Brink
© pic Zyna

'RAPE' TUSSEN 4...

Fluister hul drif...sag
Grynsend brute gelag
Wie het onheil verwag
Wie sou dit verander in prag?

Tussen 4 'rape' mure
Tel ek wrede ure
Geblus ewig my liefdes vure?
Gedwong tot stilte selfs die bure

Wie durf tog vertel
My geseling hierdie HEL!!
Wreed...en jy is n pel?
Niemand glo my in sel

Daardie 4 sal ook swyg
As hul oor my buig
My eer van my steel
Nooit weer is ek heel??

Bo n Stil getuiens
Breek tog oop die bye~nes!!!

deur Dawid Brink
© pic Marinus

'14) 'ROADBLOCK'

Hey! Wat se geit
Dieri pad is wyt
Dè smyt hom eit!
Soma terwyl djy flyt

Die pad hy drai syt
'Roadblock' hoe dan nou
Djy mit djou oogge grou
Klap djy my, my'se ore tyt

Net aan djou been gevat
Toe ik skyf in n laer rat
Met my'se neus ten die mat
Hir djy! Djou kwaie kat!

Hoe sal ik mak om viby te kom
Twee, 3,6 mak ik n som
Dres my we ik klap vi hom

Djou 'gorgious' blondie bom

Weer leer ik my'se les
Skop uit dai blok...die pes
n 'Roadblock' woes ou Tes
Keer my hir en da met n mes!

deur Dawid Brink
© pic Marinus

12 UUR..BLOED en 'n KRUIS

12 uur het bloedig geslaan
Deur donker dae, doods dae heen
Twee maal...ja twee maal kraai 'n haan
Bitter lood-trane is daar geween

12 uur deur my bloedig waas
Neuwels van skuldlas...soos dit my pas?
Na Sy kruis my spoedig haas
Laat my vertel van die hel wat werklik was

12 uur breek oop soos bloed
Hoe sal ek vergoed, my sonde...Hy't geboet
Ek waardig smaak heerlik Sy vergifnis soet
Staan ek voor hom in nuwe moed

12 uur Hy 'n bloedige gemors
Vas aan die kruis gespyker vir my
Tot drie uur worstel met die dood die Hemel Vors

Ganser aarde in donkerte gehul...sonde swaar...Hy ly

'Skeur rotse! Breek breek aarde oop'
'Dit is Volbring!!!' dit bring geheel al nuwe hoop!!!

deur Dawid Brink
© pic Mellet

ENGEL VAN GOD'se AARDE

Zyna...vryna...pyna!...myna?
Sy wil my vi di wêreld wys! EINA!
Jou krulle-bol blonde geraamde gelaat
Hartjie teer...wyd oop, dis wa-mee jy praat

Prag dogter jonk en moi! Ma se trots!
Verhoudings geskoei op Jesus ons standvastig Rots
Weerlooses...verlate mensies te help...joueie kos
'Angel of the earth' roep Chobè en ons jou mos

Maaarr as dit dan stil word rondom jou
Die hartseer en pyn...gryp Sy arms na jou...toe te...vou

Snik en huil dan aan Sy bors, niemand ander kan troos
Oor n verlore gebroke wêreld...so broos...

Rig Hy die lam knie wat struikel weer op!
Sy Liefdes-Bloed sal diè bose werke dood, dood stop!!!

deur Dawid Brink
© pic Zyna van der Merwe

JOU NAAM IN BLOU

Oë so blou soos die lug, skree ek jou naam
Skitter sterre stil juig dan saam
Asems snak...word, word sommer vlak
'STUNNING' ma 'slim blond' haar oë in my hart haak

Jou glimlag klim in my siel
Harte breek uit in jubel se riel
Dans ek op die son gryp na die maan
Gedra op die vleuels in die sterre se baan

Verruklik 'sexy' gesofistikeerde vrou

Geurig soos goeie wyn...ewig smag ek na jou
Beneweld van liefde ja!... In n dwaal v passie
Laat jy bekoorlik my, swewe in n bedwelmde fantasie

n 'Gorgious' bondeltjie 'gesofisticated fun'
'Racin hearts of men...you have on the run'
'after all...Alet...my heart is set'
'I cannot rest till our hearts in unison met'

deur Dawid Brink
© pic Alet

VREUGDE VROU!

Vreugde vrou...Jesus...het jou
Met prag en skoonheid geseënd...en...Hy wou
Jou by Homself hê, ma aan ons geleen

Mooi skitter oë in bewondering getooi
Lippe sag pruil in n glimlag...lig...roi
Pêrel fuweel jou vels gelaat

Kartelend raaf swart jou hare krans val
Omvou omraam asemrowende gesig in kontras, dit sal

Sag Lyne strakies vloeiend lig in kleure pastel

Verheerlik Hom Sy Voete Betraand met hare dan was
Oorgegee Sy skitter glans weerspieël, weg elke las
Vreugd bruid vir manlief 'handsome'...
soos jy Jesus VREUGDEVOL UITSTRAAL

deur Dawid Brink
© pic Juanita

IN SKADU TINT

Skadu vlokkies soos getinte sneeu
Kartel gedeelt uit jou sonne gelaat
Hoog bo jou, eensaam... swerf n meeu
Skoonheid uitgedeel aan jou sonder maat

Groen...grou...lower poele van 'bliss'
Röi...möi lippies möi...Röi
Wange 'velvety' sag, my aanvoel sal jou mis
Lig in n glimlag stralend in getöi

Goud-kleurig jou hare tint, Jou prag-beeld omstraal
Toon my jou hart, gelap uit op jou mou
Jou 'beauti' skadu profiel...in my kop die maal

Red jy n gebroke kruik...met tere liefde omvou

Gewaar, in möi n oog kaleideskoop van n reënboog
Jo, Lee en Nin towerland ver, ver land van ys
Sangeeta opgetof in lof van 'Astairè' op verhoog
Luister ope mond wyd in hul se hys

Armani kode van jou na my geursel-grotte se bode
Jasmyn, lemoen bloeisel vermeng in jou geur..
My hart ruk smag smag in my nagtlik node
Verdrink ekke in effe soutig muskus meer en meer

n Storie in bloedig of lag van 'Grietjie' herleef uit haar pen
weer en weer..

deur Dawid Brink
© pic C'Mor

LIEFDES VERLANGE BESKRYF

Hanli...Hanli Leach, heerlik daar oppi 'beach'
Laafend en vraend jou woorde rol
Soos die branders breek penne vol
'Not hard, Not hard you to reach'

Dig woorde ledig dai mooi, mooi hart...
Gebore getoë gegryp soms uit diepe smart.,.
Letters val bymekaar maak tot woorde wat tart
Broose liefde verspeel en dan weer is ons heel

Swart donkerte my liefd- verlatendheid-skimme
Terg my skemer nag, deur stad...tot deur n grag
Arms vol van verlange, koel soel my wange
Gryp skadu-skimme sotte in diep grotte uit grimme

Hang-on in there! I know all is not fair!
Flikker liefdes vlam in elk hart op te hang
Paapie na Vlinder so ontdooi, in klampe vasgevang

Afgeskud die droom sindroom...vervuld die verlang

Dan my pen lê voor haar, stil...stiller... dan n muis

deur Dawid Brink
© pic Hanli

DORRE, DORRE SANDSPOKE

Dorre sandspoke gereed in verbete geveg
My 4 by 4 staan n prys in hulle weg
Bleek buig geblykte ridders, staan ferm op hul reg...
Omhoë geboë bekruip rond in n kring

Ongenadiglik brand die son verskroeiend neer...
Saam, saam vorm hul heg heilig vyand's band
Meester oor Meester...sluiter deur die sand
As die skadu's daal, mòre word weer gaan haal

Ons sand-skimme breek soms wreed uit
Deur vasberade gebitte roggelend fluit
Asems wat jaag soekend na jou buit
Verskeur tot dorre, dorre beendere lê ons suid

Maak-Spoke lê ons skoon lam
Hul prys 'n 4 by 4 en...en n 'stunning' San!

deur Dawid Brink
© pic Leanin~Lee

GELIEFD' MELLET...

Mellet Moll...uit jou pen...woorde rol...
Snags tot laat-aand by 'Café al' la Poem' inni Mall
Legionaire...Storm...spreek uit jou hart so woordvol

Woord Wiggelaar somtyd 'stunning' somtyd swaar
Pen en Ink gryp vas jou woorde...waar?
Waar Woorde Werk... uit jou vaardig pen sy merk

Lizette, Hanli, Hester en ek Sit stil saam by die hek
'Cheer' jou ewig woorde dans om jou plek
Ons siele onuitwisbaar, waar woorde wat aanhou trek...

Waar Woorde...Weemoedig...Ekstase...gee ons n 'trill'
Trek ons hoër onse spul, verslawend soos n dagga pil
Ysters formules, 'mechanics'...lief en leed...jy...weet?

Bundel na bundel...geurig, spoeg jy uit soos n automaat

Legendes soos Breyten, Ingrid, van Wijk Louw...voeg net jou by ou Maat

Deel Waar Woorde Wat geil groei tot Saad...

deur Dawid Brink
© pic Mellet Moll

JESUS en ons SPECIAL..SPECIALS

Jy's...uit God se hart...n SPECIAL SPECIAL!
Al die ander ok sooo special
Ma...Jy...Jy's...n SPECIAL SPECIAL!!

Pienkie ka tinkie Jesus se Blinkie
Feetjie ka seetjie engel se Vlerkie
Richie ka fietsie Jesus se rein Hartjie
Siyabonga ka wonga Jesus se Songa
Zellie ka pellie ons Koning se Vellie

Hemel kinders ons geleen
Bring Koning Jesus se seen
Hy laat pragtig glimlaggies reën

Die wind speel liedtjies deur jul hare
Pragtig mooi, mooi Sonne skare

Engele Maatjie sag soos katjies geleen vir jare

Jy Piekie! Jesus en ons se SPECIAL SPECIAL!
Jy Feetjie! Jesus en ons se SPECIAL SPECIAL!
Jy Richie! Jesus en ons se SPECIAL SPECIAL!
Jy Siyabonga! Jesus en ons se SPECIAL SPECIAL!
Jy Zellie! Jesus en ons se SPECIAL SPECIAL!

deur Dawid Brink
© pic Cathy

DIE WET VAN DIE GEES…(Rom 6,7,8)

Keer...op...keer faal...
Ou...ou sonde herhaal?
Wanneer sal ons...LEER?
Probeer ma weer n keer...

Ons së...ons's ma net...mens
Llllliieeef ek dit...of ma n wens?
So gevaarlik na aan die kant
'My Sonde' geskryf in die sand...

Ag! Heer! Tog n laaste keer
LIEG ek AL, AL WEER?
AG! Wie red my uit my nood!
'Desperado' vlees, vlees jy moet dood!!!

O! Hoe Heerlik! Opgewonde ek bewe...
Diè Wet van die Gees van die Lewe...
In Christus Jesus maak my VRY!!!
Waarom sal ek in my vuil sonde LY???
deur

Dawid Brink ©

IN MY SKEMER...

In die skemer van my...geloof
My rug, ruk, rukkend in n boog
Maak ek dit net, net...roos-kleurig die lug...
Betraand buig dit my ruk, ruk rukkend in n sug...

Blaar en blom aan my horisonne verdwyn
Elk minuut gryp diep my...kwynend...kwyn...
Sy groot liefde heerlik skoon en rein
Sonde-bok wreed SY sonne lyn

Taan SY Heerlik Godlikbeeld...my eie waan
Gly weg! My hemel reg?
Vergeet tog so gou SY doodsbenou geveg...
Hy het Versoen...die vyand uitgeklee...dis gedaan!

Heer...MASHIACH vergeef sewentig sewe maal
Rig my opnuut...vul met U Gees...DIÈ sal my nooit faal!

deur Dawid Brink ©

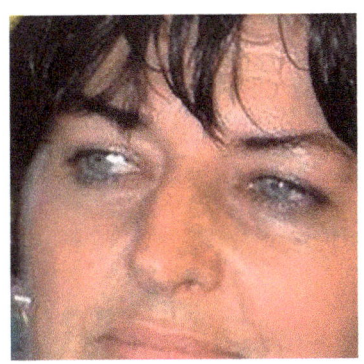

MOOI SPORE...

Spore mooi...van lief dan leed...
DIÈ...het...jou...nöit, nöit vergeet
Oë sag blou...tog mooi grou
Blydskap te sien...net om jou

Mooi Spore mooi...van heerlik swaarkry so straf..
Kleurvol lewe n nikkerbol...dan by n oop graf..
Seerrrr...in...oomblikke van blou..
'Exquisite' karakter en prag...dan my inbou....

Heerlike Spore...van lekkkerrrr en 'bliss'
Wie sou öit, öit jou draaie, draaie wis?
Diep Spore diep...sal...laat...jou gemis
Wille wêreld gryp jy aan uitbundig met lus!

Glorie Skepper jy't gehoor 'Wel gedaan'!
Wawiel Spore deur Hom ingetrap...soos deur Hom gebaan!

deur Dawid Brink ©

MÖIER dan MÖI

Möier...dan...Möi...
Lippe sag en röi...
Möier Ja!...dan Möi!

Möier dan...prag Möi
Oë wat lag...fuweel sag
Möier prag...dan...Möi!

Möier 'Explosive' Möi
Raaf swart lokke kartel...
Möier O! My hart!...so Möi!!

Möier 'Stunnin' Möi
Melkwit pêrelbyters skitter

Möier 'Gorgiously'!...Möi...

Möier dan Möi
Siele-vensters 'declare' sprankelend siel-vuur
Möier! Verdomp!...möier...

deur Dawid Brink
© pic Annelize

JESUS dan EK

Ek...n Veldblommetjie… verfraai my William…se hoed
Hy't so mooi gevra...vol, vol manne-moed
Jou geur walm vars, vrolik op, jy blom stip op tyd...
Skoonheid en praal jou verhaal wyd tot syt

Oë sag, deur biggel traan venster, dan skater lag!
Groot groei my hart vol liefde klop...vi seun en pop
Jesus liefdes Koning Hy, Hy bring heerlik loning
Ontsaglik Sy Koningkryk, versier word ons woning

Gekleeft Sy skouer dra Hy my drog pak...tot ek is ouer
Deurskeurde hande wond, spykers stop sonde geskryf in my sand…
Den Bloede geanker Jesus voet, rem my waar ek land

Oordonderend ek die bose, grote oorwinning van
Sy kant

Vuil kop-gedagtes gereining...deurklief Sy dorings...diep in
gesteek
Wrede spies boor My Sy… ontsluit water, bloed die breek
Vergruis kliphart van my… Sy spiespunt laat my week
Trooster O! Gees vul my… Lieft, wysheid en krag ek, ek diè leek

Gerustend ge-eik, helend glory Sy Woord
'WEES NIE BEVREES NIE'!!!
Galm dit uit oord tot oord...

deur Dawid Brink
© pic Riana Munnik

LEONIE

Diep, diep my peins...sou Hy hier my gewaar?
Hier teen 'Oue heer' sit ek daar
Die lewe is lig...tog is dit swaar
Sit en peins diep ek oor, oor... n laer

Jare staan hy al hier
Ja, ja sit ek en tuur
Verwonderd Hy't my gemaak ek Sy praal
Kom Hy seker...seker my haal

My hare val uit in n dos

Nooit! Nee nooit! Sal Hy my los
Kosbaarder as enig iets is Hy!
Bloed, Bloed vloei vir my, uit Sy Sy

Vergenoegd rus ek in jou koel
Ja! Ja! Hy weet dat ek diep voel
Die pad was so lank…en berg steil
Maar God…God steeds my heil

deur Dawid Brink
© pic Leonie

SANNIE SONNEBLOM

Sannie...sleep...sewe...sak...sout...
Sonder...sy...sy...së...sy...sleep...swaar!
Het jy haar op die swaar sleepsel spoor gewaar?
Met, met die fraaie son van blom in haar...haar

Swoeg sy vaaannn soggenvroeg tot laat
Ten wind dan weer...kintjies ten di kwaat
Sonika dra..ja sy dra Pinki rond in...haar hart
Soms is dit...woes...soms...is dit...ssswwart!!

Röikop...hemelkind wat my wëreld eens het verhelder
Doods kloue haar met kake gegryp...gekelder...
Sy leef vört, vört in passie van San gewillig hand
Haar rusplek...knus by Hom, toegegooi...in kombers van sand

Haar goue krans vars in, in blare trans
Omring voedsel saad...geveerde vriend my ou maat
'Eet My Vlees en...drink My Bloed'
So...SO...word San en ek eintlik ge...voed

RUSPLEK! Rusplek...ook jy...ek? Oplaas
VADER...TEEN SY BORS..IN SY RUS...STAAN EK VERBAAS

deur Dawid Brink
© pic Sannie

SOET MELODIE

Wollerige watte wat wolk kombers uitsprei
Gedek waar wolke warm krul...feë dans op uitlei...
Vlerk geritsel bondelende haarlokke tuimel na benee
Kry n koets...kry...kry vi my n perd en slee

Chello klank kabbelend klink strelend soet
Bruis binne my tot n 'crescendo' binne my bloed
Betowerende blydskap 'blast' streel my gemoed
Vibrator simfonie van klank vul my bruisend bloed

Soet, soetste melodie van estatiese borreling
Tower jou wasbeeld en prag gelaat...uitsonderling
Broos...Breeekbaar...sag, gly jy Feë Prinses
Op maat van wonder strelend melody...'so impress'

Sonne silver straal verdwyn kwynend...
My wese dra soetste, soetste melody...tot my siel... reinigend!!

deur Dawid Brink © pic Lizette

RUAAN…MY 'SPECIAL' 8

Agt vleg in tekens deur Jesus Naam…
Drie siele…ek, pa…en jy ver-bind ons oneindig saam..
Jesus het jou in ons eie prent vir 25jr geraam
n Stukkie hemel, hemel wat…wat min verstaan…

Die 'Nootlot' het, het jou blind by ons gelaat?
Oë van die hart, hart het jou sien gemaak…
Jou vreugde borrel gedurig uitbindig oor ons uit
Stig ons…hande vou saam…Skepper onse dank is LUID!

Jou 'handsome' beeld gelaat, my nöit verlaat…
Koning Jesus ons is seer…maar bewaar gelaat
Agt! Agt!! Agt!!!..maal merk uit ons goue lyn…
Deurweek ons lewens draad, Jesus verlig al die pyn!

Jou gebrek byna, byna deur ons, ons ongemerk…
Dan breek…bars n jubel kreet…deur die stukkend verskeur!!
Glorie! Glorie liggame…Sy opstanding Jesus…my leer

Sy kosbaar Bloed ons versoen...Sy Gees so ons versterk!!!

deur Dawid Brink © pic Riana
Opgedra aan Ruaan se 25st verjaarsdag 13 Okt 2011

RÖIRÖK...RÖI

Röi-Rok Röi...wie, wie het jou in my hart kom ströi?

Repe...repe bloedig uit, uit gekerf seer RöiRok Röi

Jou gelaat uit geëts...verdomp so verskriklik, verskriklik möi!

*Wreed..soet, .soet..wreed, diep gryp jou klampe diep..elk in sy
söi*

Super krisp...krisp snak koel...kraak, kraak...so vars!

Vrolik...eg vroulik, verruklik uit jou kas...sou jy mars...

Bol...lekka, lekka bol blyd skap-vreugde...ströi sonder maat

Verrasende goue strale om-arm jou prag gelaat

'Baby, baby want to make you mine'...weerklinkend op maat

*'More aged...No! More experienced' na gelang die tyd Ha!
Ha!*

*Dis reg!...haar na Töorberg gevat...sy reg vi my... op n tiekji...
Na! Na!*

*Jy weet net wat te sê...Lag met my...'soulmates'...bedoel ek...
Ja! Ja!*

*Vergenoegdsame...'explosive' borrelend vreugde...eintlik
'bliss' Lae! Op Lae!!*

deur Dawid Brink © pic Michelle v Staden

IN DIE LIG AGTER JOU

In die lig...Lig agter jou Strale Vrou..
Sien ek die Wonderlig...wat wik...van jou!
Skoonste jou oog belewe geensins...jou Strale Krans...
Betowerings Lig...soos jou hart se dans...

Uit jou skone binneste breek...Helderste Lig...
Lig uit jou Lig...penitreer my dieps te stig!
My hart se vlug...vlug voort gly op jou Ligstrale nou
Jou oorweldig, helderste Lig...dra my op vlerke lug so blou!

Glorie-Lig wonderbaar breek oor jou gesigsgelaat
Jesus liefdes Lig...die Lig...Sy Lig jou vrygemaak!
Verblindend Lig dring tot diep binne jou diepste diep...
Plofkrag sterker as tien duisende atombomme...die reinig diep

Tog...sag skeur die Lig...omsingel, verban my duisternis
Tot een kaal-nakend vlamme wildernis!!

Vrymakende glorie, ewige Lig..lok my na nuwe plig
Verweelsag jou kroning dansend heerlik...dig...

Verlustigend verdrink ek myself in jou Glorie Lig...
Bars dit verspulend...vermorsend...oor ons...Sy Glory Lig!!!

deur Dawid Brink
© pic Marietha

BERG VELD-SMUL

Op klip sit drie musketiers di verte in en tuur...
Smul aan hoender boutjies sonder...bier...
Wors saam eierbroodjie voor wuifend gras
Karel, Thea en ek...kibbel oor boom-se-tak en bas...
Kramp op kramp...Ouch!! Mmmmm...in my voet se hy...
Moet ek Vryf en vryf en vryf se sy...
O hy 'n ni mee da ni
Glimlagend herinner hy ons dis di 'missing' ene
Grinnik ons droee laggies van verstaan...so inni ry...

Bo-op die berg vry, skoon is die lug..
Ver kan ons sien, Alwyn en krans voel in vlug...
Twaalf verskillende bome...Kiepersol...wag-n-bietjie...
Onder die paar bekend...dan treffend die liedjie...
Moses en Abraham onder bespreking diep...
Een diepste nederig...die ander vader van geloof,
sal jy jou kind se lig dan self uitdoof... ??
Eier en pomelo's ryg ons saam in...
Jakkals en bobbejaan bespreekte sin...
Wens vervuld, kuns-trap weer boeiend die natuur.
Nie duidelik soos van ouds steeds brand sy vuur.
Verlange so effe gesus, staaltjies uit di verte...
Verluister ons ons...kou jelly-babes sonder sterte...
Siels-verkwikt, son-versadigt huiswaarts keer
Dankbaar...vreugd gevuld, ons Heer se gegewe dag
Jesus, Moses, Elia...op die berg vind ons krag...
diepversadiging gevoed ons gees en sinne weer

deur: Dawid Brink
© pic Dawid

MY NOTE FANTASIE

Hier knus waar ek droomverlore lê
Dol verlief...wil ek dan net sê
Met noot en klank
Klawer...kitaar...klastenette...klinkel

Sou ek prag kleure in klanke kon sien
Hoe möi sou dit sigbaar speel...
Möiste Groen v middel C...
Röi vi hoogste E...rangskik in klawerkas
Git swart...banaal...di...bas

Op kleure en note sweef jy na my
Ontplof my hart heeel vry!!!
Die note op die skaal gly…
Gryp na jou met kleurvolle note bly!!

Opgewonde kleur-klanke drae jou skoonheid ver
Note uitgeknip van krinkel-papier…met…n skêr
Draaitjies en swaaitjies …jy met 'flaïr'
In n waas op skone melodie sweef ek en jy..
…….'not a care'…

Deur Dawid Brink
© Pic Lizzi

MY RUG NA JOU

Met my seep-gewas...rug na jou
Waaroor het ek...het ek nou weer met jou getrou
Fasineerend is di kosbare prentji my vrou
Soepel hand geklem...oor kruis in jou arm se waai...
My gedagte gang opgewonde jou beeld laai...

Onsigbare krane laat vloei gedagtes deur di bad
Op die rant van die erde-skat sit n swarte kat...
Haartjies preuts uitlokkend in n bollatjie verbind
Wyd jou knieggies vul laafenes in die buig gevind

Ge-ets verruklike soel lyn van jou lyf
Lokkend deur die skeure van my ruik...
Kon ek ure terug my hande nog voel op jou buik...
Wasem vars, verkwikend geure ruk in my brein diep geskryf
Ewig onvergeetlik 'stunning' skilder...lyf...ruik...buik...skryf!!!!

Deur Dawid Brink
© Pic Wilmien

OU TAFELBERG VERTEL..

Ek Möiste ou berg gedek met my mantel...wit
Gedek vi Gode Seun .. aan te sit
Moeg en tam na die lange rit
Sta Ingele algar möi te dient in gelit

Plat is my blad ek is Zuiderland se skat..
By Sy Omdraai kom vind Hy Sy lafenis
Noorde se roepe..haastig..tog gerus..kossies te vat
Op hierrie ou Kaapse Hemels rug.. pragse erfnis

Jan en Vasco kon my praal nie weerstaan
Nòg Dias en selfse Dingiswayo en Dingaan!
Hy was oppad ver uit die Noorde
Verby Natal met al sy goue strand oorde

Bloed kleur my nat voeten-ent

Waar sal Boer, Brit,Kaaskop en Köi hom na wend

Geloofshelde ontvlug son godsvader se brandstapel..valbyl
lem

Hul het die ware Liefdevol God geken

Menig verhaal speel af voor my reènt en wolke kleed

Hartseer teem di slawe klok en vryheidstryders in tronke wreed

Verrys voor my, vryheids-stryde in ongekende wreedheid... tot
prag-skoonheid

'Rainbow Nation'. ..gaan hy homself op die plein ophang in
bleekheid???

Een Heilig Bloed het my broeder-berg eens gevlek

Moria, Zion's..Golgotha! God my Skepper uitgestrek!

Sy kruis stamp in sy rotsgewand..uitgesprei Sy hand..

Roep na die vegtend wesens voor my Kleed-Berg ..dek my'se
skand

deur Dawid Brink
© prentjie Heritage legkaart

ONS BLOED VOED??

Ek hoor nog die perde hoef gedruis
Walg-kruit slaan op in my neus soos n vuis
Makkers se doodskreet roggel nog in die wind
Sal my Lief met haar kappie en voorskoot my bloed kan vind?

Gestrooi...bevlek dit my woorde, ek was nog kind
Speels ek en Klaas in die spruit klei-osse.hul is .blind
Ons moes kleilat mar.. nou meng onse bloed
Wat opbou tot n gedruis soos die Oranje in vloed

Oseane van bloed kom lê ongemerk in die Thems
Verf hul Buckingham Palace, mee te verfraai?
Vrot stank breek deur tot voor God se troon
Duiwels lag, spot vertrap en hoon

Ek ruik gebrande mielie-oes en weidings gras
Plaashuis ook dier smeul met roet en bloed
Skryf die kakies ons geskiedenis vreesloos vas
Hul kinders in goue borde eet ons vlees..drink ons bloed

Ons vroue en kinder sterf in konsentrasie uitgeteer
Doodsroggel wit en swart kan ek uithou steeds…meer
'Royal Empire' is uit hul 'boer en kaffir' se stof en bloed gebou
bloed-goud…bloed-diamant, pruik 'trots' op kroon en hals van
n vrou

'War Crimes' wie van die Lords sal daarvoor boet
Geeërde Churchill, Barnato, Cecil John versuip in ons skatte…

deur Dawid Brink © pic Dawid

BOERIN (n wens)

As jy hier teen my kom lê...
Skaap-geur en seer spier..dan net sê..
Balsem van Gilead 'kom O lafenis'
Spoel verfrissend reiningende mis

Diepe hartseer spore...stadig...taan
Diè lewe het sy merk aan my gedaan
Laaste stuiptrekkings 'wanneer' sal dit los?'
'Sy greep op my strot!' n geslepe vos!

Planne verruis breek deur die neuwels van stof

Op die horison kom n ruiter aangery
Pronkstert die hings se trippel maak my bly

As ek in sy arms stout…kan rus…
Sy lippe teen my slaap voel kus
Teen sy bree harig bors my lyf kan vlei
Rus 'my wêreld' stadig...polsend in dan gly...

deur Dawid Brink
© pic 'wilde Wilmien'

LAASTE RIT 'GHOST-RIDER'

n Ruiter skim op die röi horison...
Om hom berg, krans en hoog bo pruik n blom
DonkerHoek sy hart verlang...pynlik kramp...
Lyndrade lê plat...geen skaap of bees op kamp...

DiepKloof water is soet, dik loop dit deur haar bloed
Vier kinders...sy in liefde verlaat...di het sy gevoed
Hoe skep jy na soveel droeë jare weer moed...
Gestroop van huppelende lam, bokspring kalf...hoop?

Ruisende wind vlinder deur haar hare..

Blom,das en bok buig hoflik soos vir n skare...
Hoef...Halter...Helder, Klap...Kinkel...Koggel...
Klok helder skater lag speel deur krans~prag...

Coco George se oë blits vure en vlam
'GostRider' se sweep swiep
en krans antwoord in weergalm
Bloots sy een met hom...Coco George! Spiere bult

Groot en Kragtig, breek hy in matige gallop..
Dink NET! n Kas Cas'tles..hy's?...sy's?...baie wild...?

Traan-Druppels vorm met die was van sy kers...
Verlangend sit en smag ek...ek skryf n vers...
'CowGirl'...my hart ruk...pluk ek jou om...
Oë wat laggend my speels-tart...'GostRider'! Ek's stom!

deur Dawid Brink
© pic Saline

********************END*****************